The Bungler

The Bungler

By Molière

Translated into English verse
by Richard Wilbur

THEATRE COMMUNICATIONS GROUP
NEW YORK
2010

The Bungler is published by Theatre Communications Group, Inc., 520 Eighth Avenue, 24th Floor, New York, NY 10018–4156

This project is funded by the Sidney E. Frank Foundation.

This publication is made possible in part with public funds from the New York State Council on the Arts, a State Agency.

TCG books are exclusively distributed to the book trade by Consortium Book Sales and Distribution.

LIBRARY OF CONGRESS CATALOGING-IN-PUBLICATION DATA
Molière, 1622–1673.
[Etourdi. English]
The bungler / by Molière ; translated into English verse by Richard Wilbur.
—1st ed.
p. cm.
ISBN 978-1-55936-351-8
I. Wilbur, Richard, 1921– II. Title.
PQ1832.E7E5   2010
842'.4—dc22   2010014454

Cover design by Chip Kidd
Cover image: Burstein Collection/Corbis
Text design and composition by Lisa Govan

First Edition, May 2010

For my son Christopher

Contents

Introduction

The Bungler (*l'Étourdi*) was Molière's first verse comedy. For his troupe, which had been touring the provinces for a decade, the play's successful premiere at Lyons in 1655 was a crucial moment in its progress toward Paris. The same play was the first offering of Molière's company when, sponsored by the king's brother, it began its Parisian career at the Petit-Bourbon in 1658. Once again, the piece was wildly successful. Molière offered it frequently thereafter, and since his death it has been presented hundreds of times, with such great comic actors as Coquelin in the part of Mascarille. All of which may make one wonder why *The Bungler*—which Victor Hugo considered the best of Molière's comedies—is so seldom mentioned in discussions of its author's works.

The answer, I think, is that (apart from comic timing, wit and poetic genius) the virtues of this hilarious five-acter are not those of Molière's major phase. *The Bungler* does not depict the manners of Molière's society. It does not create complex characters, like Alceste and Orgon. It has no such artful plot structure as *The Misanthrope* possesses and no such thematic weight as we find, for instance, in *The Learned Ladies'* consideration of the place of art and erudition in everyday life. What *The Bungler* is, is a zestful and sustained performance in the vein of that Italian popular comedy with which Molière and all of mid-seventeenth-century France were familiar. It derives from the *commedia dell'arte*, a form of theater in which stock characters improvised within sketchy outlines or "scenarios," and from such plays as Nicolò Barbieri's *l'Inavvertito* (which was, in fact, a "scenario" elaborated into a prose script). Molière makes plain his adaptive intentions by laying the action in Messina, by giving his characters such Italianate names as Pandolfe and by evoking the stock figures and situations of *commedia*: avaricious and domineering old men, young lovers separated by obstacles, cunning servants who spin intrigues in the lovers' interest. *The Bungler*, which with vigor and invention transports all this into the high mode of verse comedy, is the French enhancement of an Italian genre.

As Act One begins, it is convenient to know that a beautiful young woman named Célie, who was part of a gypsy band, has lately been given by the gypsies to a rich old man named Trufaldin as security for a loan. It's in that sense that she can be described as a "slave" or "captive." The play's impetuous young hero, Lélie, who formerly vied with a young man named Léandre for the favor of a girl named Hippolyte, has spied Célie and transferred his affections to her. Learning now that Léandre, too, is smitten by Célie, and is once again his rival, he turns for strategic help to his clever valet Mascarille, who proceeds to cook up the first of many schemes.

All of that, despite the novel feature of a pawned heroine, feels like a standard opening situation for a comedy: we know that it will be the business of the play to unite Lélie and his Célie; we suspect that Célie will prove to be no gypsy, but a girl of gentle birth; we count on Mascarille to hatch some great intrigue whereby to win Célie for his master, though we are not quite sure why it should take five acts for that to be accomplished. Five acts prove to be necessary because, even when made a part of Mascarille's cunning plots—as initially he is not—the rash and blundering Lélie somehow manages to torpedo them, one after another. That is the distinctive repeated joke of *l'Étourdi*, and it does not become tiresome. A chief delight of the play is to witness Mascarille's resilient ability to think up ever-new devices, and to see how the plot will arrange for them to be frustrated, again and again, by the intended beneficiary.

An eighteenth-century French editor of *l'Étourdi* found the play morally disquieting, and there is no question that it toys throughout with our ambivalent feelings about deception and fraud. Mascarille, who tirelessly strives to be "the most glorious trickster in the town," and who has the longest part in all of Molière, is massively central to that theme, yet there is scarcely a character in the piece who does not have moments, venial or otherwise, of guileful behavior. Célie, playing the seeress in order to deceive Trufaldin, shows a natural aptitude for intrigue. Hippolyte engages Mascarille to scheme for her success in love, and a plot of Mascarille's is readily embraced by Pandolfe. Anselme achieves a sly counter-swindle in retrieving his purse. Léandre attempts to abduct Célie under cover of a masquerade. As for the hero Lélie, he begs his valet to aid him with plots and ruses, takes part in some of them, soliloquizes in extenuation of a fraud (Act Two, Scene 1), and pulls a hoax of his own (Act Two, Scenes 10–11) of which he is very proud. A comedy, however, is not a court of law, and the play gives its young lovers a blanket absolution on the principle that all's fair in love. Furthermore, they all have attractive and redeeming qualities: Célie is noble and honorable, Hippolyte is magnanimous, Léandre is a good sport and the warm, naive and spontaneous Lélie is gallant in rescuing a stranger from false arrest. In Mascarille, by contrast, the main motive for duplicity is not love but *amour-propre* and a need to be the smartest of outsmarters; he is a diabolical inverter of values, who describes his chicanery as "virtue" and aspires to be the acknowledged *imperator* of rascals. Outside of this play, he would be deplorable; within its comic precincts he provides wit and irrepressibility and a tang of the sinister. One reason why his intricate and dubious plottings are purely enjoyable is that they come to nothing, and that the denouement—the disclosures, recognitions and happy pairings of the fifth act—is, after all, none of his doing.

John Dryden once freely reworked for the stage a prose translation of *l'Étourdi* by the Duke of Newcastle, adding much other material, borrowed or fresh, and some Restoration coarseness. The result, *Sir Martin Mar-All* (1667), was judged by Samuel Pepys, who saw it again and again, to be "the best comedy ever was wrote." An eighteenth-century prose rendering by Baker and Miller, like the nineteenth-century version by Charles Heron Wall, was worthy but not stageworthy, and what follows is intended as the second playable treatment of *l'Étourdi* in English. I hope also to have done a good and exact translation for the contemporary reader. I've sought to be strictly faithful to the original in all respects—in sense, in tone and in verse form—and it may amuse the reader to know of a couplet whose punning character stumped me. In Act Five, Scene 5, Mascarille has disguised himself as a German-accented Swiss landlord, in order to deceive Andrès. Lélie inopportunely appears and, in Andrès's presence, addresses his valet by name: "Well, Mascarille! No one would ever guess / That it was you in that outlandish dress." Mascarille's reply is:

> *Moi souis ein chant t'honneur, moi non point Maquerille:*
> *Chai point fentre chamais le fame ni le fille.*

That might be translated:

> Vy do you say I am a *Maquereau*?
> I sell no vimmen here, I'll haf you know.

Unfortunately, though my great Funk and Wagnalls (1913) gives "maquereau" as an English word meaning "pimp" or "procurer," the word is not to be found in any of the more recent dictionaries I have consulted. The *Shorter OED* allows "mackerel" (meaning procurer), but once again the term seems not to have much currency. For intelligibility's sake, and because Mascarille has already, in Scene 3, held forth on the propriety of his establishment, I have settled for:

> Vy do you call me Mackerel? I don't vish
> Zat you make fun of me und call me fish.

Purists may choose, in reading my translation, to substitute the "maquereau" couplet; actors will doubtless find that, for their audiences, the fish joke is clearer and funnier.

For general encouragement in my translating of Molière, I wish to thank Jacques Barzun, William Jay Smith and Sonja Haussmann Smith. And for his specific suggestion that I undertake *The Bungler*, I am grateful to Albert Bermel. My wife Charlotte has as always given me her good and patient counsel.

—RW
Cummington, Massachusetts, 1999

The Bungler

Characters

LÉLIE (lay-LEE), Pandolfe's son
CÉLIE (say-LEE), Trufaldin's slave
MASCARILLE (mah-ska-REE), Lélie's valet
ANSELME (ahn-SELM), Hippolyte's father
HIPPOLYTE (ee-po-LEET), Anselme's daughter
TRUFALDIN (tru-fal-DAN), an old man
PANDOLFE (pahn-DOLF), Lélie's father
LÉANDRE (lay-AHN-druh), a young man of good family
ANDRÈS (ahn-DRACE), a supposed gypsy
ERGASTE (air-GHAST), a friend of Mascarille's
A MESSENGER
TWO COMPANIES OF MASQUERADERS

Place

A public square in Messina, Sicily.

A Note to Directors and Actors

The two names Albert and Horace are frequently spoken in *The Bungler,* and should be pronounced in a more or less French manner as "al-BEAR" and "o-RAHSS."

Act One

Scene 1

Lélie.

LÉLIE

Well then, Léandre, get ready for a fray!
We'll see which one of us will win the day—
Which one will thwart the other's longing for
The heavenly creature whom we both adore.
Muster your forces, and be on your guard;
I mean to press the attack, and press it hard!

Scene 2

Lélie, Mascarille.

LÉLIE

Ah, Mascarille!

MASCARILLE

Sir?

LÉLIE

I'm in a dreadful state;
My love life's always being spoiled by fate:
Léandre now loves Célie, so that although
I've a new love, I have the same old foe.

MASCARILLE

Léandre loves Célie!

LÉLIE

Adores her; yes.

MASCARILLE

Bad luck.

LÉLIE

It is; imagine my distress.
Yet I'd be foolish to despair or doubt;
With your help, I feel sure of winning out.
You're full of clever schemes; your canny wit
Finds no predicament too much for it;
You are, I think, a king among valets;
In all the world . . .

MASCARILLE

Whoa! No more sugary praise.
When masters need the help of us poor hinds,
They call us paragons with brilliant minds;
But let us make some slip, and in a flash
We're stupid scoundrels who deserve the lash.

LÉLIE

Ah no, you wrong me. That's not how I behave.
But let us speak now of the lovely slave.
Tell me, could any heart, however cold,
Not melt for one so charming to behold?
Given her gentle speech and perfect face,
I think that she must come of noble race,
And that some fate has made her hide within
A humble guise her lofty origin.

MASCARILLE

A fine romantic fancy, to be sure.
But will Pandolfe approve this new amour?
He is your father, sir, or so he claims.
You know how, if you cross him, it inflames
His temper—how it makes him roar and rave
Whenever, in his view, you misbehave.
His plan is for Anselme, his neighbor, to
Bestow his daughter Hippolyte on you,
Because he thinks that only marriage can
Convert a rash youth to a sober man.
Were he to find that you refuse to wed
The girl he's chosen, and pursue instead
An unknown siren whose bewitching beauty
Has caused you to forget your filial duty,
God knows what thunders would afflict your ear,
And what long sermons you would have to hear.

LÉLIE

Enough, now! No more speeches, if you please.

MASCARILLE

Enough talk, then, of schemes and strategies!
The game's not worth the candle, and you'd be wiser . . .

LÉLIE

Thank you, I have no need of an advisor.
You know I hate advice, and a valet
Who lectures me will find it doesn't pay.

MASCARILLE

(Aside:)
He's getting angry.
(To Lélie:)
          I was but teasing, sir,
To learn how strong your amorous feelings were.
Is Mascarille some grim, censorious creature?
Am I the foe of youth and human nature?
Ah, never could you so mistake me, knowing
How jovial I am, how easygoing.
Forget the crabbèd sermons of your sire;
Be free, I say, and do as you desire.
I think that these old fogies who give tongue
To stern ideas are envious of the young;
Time having forced them to be virtuous,
They want the joys of life denied to us.
You know my gifts, sir; what would you have me do?

LÉLIE

Now, that's the talk I like to hear from you.
Well, then. My love, I find, does not despise
The passion wakened in me by her eyes.
Just now, however, Léandre said to me
That he intends to rob me of Célie:
That's why we must act quickly, now, and hatch
Some plan to make her mine with all despatch.
What trick or ruse or plot can you concoct,
Whereby my rival's purpose will be blocked?

MASCARILLE

Give me your leave to ponder that a while.
(*Aside:*)
Can I think up some useful bit of guile?

LÉLIE

Well, what's our stratagem?

MASCARILLE

I beg you, wait.
My mind can't move at such a rapid rate.
I have it: You must . . . No, you'd better not.
Still, if you went . . .

LÉLIE

Where?

MASCARILLE

No, that's a sorry plot.
But here's a notion—

LÉLIE

What?

MASCARILLE

It wouldn't do.
Perhaps—

LÉLIE

Yes?

MASCARILLE

No, that wouldn't work for you.
You might approach Anselme.

7

LÉLIE

Why? What could I say?

MASCARILLE

It's true, we'd only make things worse that way.
Yet we must have her. It's Trufaldin you must see.

LÉLIE

What for?

MASCARILLE

I'm not sure.

LÉLIE

This is too much for me;
Your dithering is more than I can stand.

MASCARILLE

Sir, if you had a well-stuffed purse in hand,
There'd be no need for us to fret and muse
On how to gain your end by some sly ruse:
We could quite simply *buy* the slave, and thus
Prevent your rival from forestalling us.
Trufaldin fears that the gypsy family
Who left her with him as security
Will cheat him, and that his loan won't be repaid.
To reimburse himself, he'll sell the maid
Gladly, for he's a miser through and through.
He'd let himself be whipped for half a sou,
And money is the god to which he kneels.
The trouble is . . .

LÉLIE

What?

MASCARILLE

That your father feels
A like regard for money, so that his treasure
Is nothing you can draw on at your pleasure.
In fact, I know of no purse in the land
Likely to open up at your command.
But let us seek to talk now with Célie,
And find out what her sentiments may be.
Right there's her window.

LÉLIE

Trufaldin, night and day,
Keeps watch upon her in a hawk-like way.
Take care.

MASCARILLE

Let's hide, then, in this corner here.
But look! What luck, that she should now appear!

Scene 3

Célie, Lélie, Mascarille.

LÉLIE

Ah, how I thank high Heaven, when I view
The heavenly charms it has bestowed on you!
Though by those eyes I have been all but slain,
What joy it is to see them once again!

CÉLIE

My heart, which hears your words with some alarm,
Would never wish my eyes to do men harm,
And if in some way they have made you grieve,
Please know that it was done without my leave.

LÉLIE

So sweetly have they pierced me that, I swear,
I glory in the precious wounds I bear,
And . . .

MASCARILLE

Sir, all this is a little too high-flown;
Our business here requires a brisker tone.
Let's quickly ask, before it is too late,
How she . . .

TRUFALDIN

(*Within the house:*)
Célie!

MASCARILLE

You see?

LÉLIE

O cruel fate!
Why must that old ape interrupt us now?

MASCARILLE

Go, hide yourself; I'll handle him somehow.

Scene 4

Trufaldin, Célie, Lélie hiding in a corner, Mascarille.

TRUFALDIN

(*To Célie:*)
What are you doing outside? As I recall,
I bade you speak to no one, no one at all.

CÉLIE

I met this honest fellow years ago,
And you need have no fears of him, I know.

MASCARILLE

Is this the famous Trufaldin?

CÉLIE

The same.

MASCARILLE

Sir, I rejoice to meet a man whose name
Is spoken everywhere with reverence.
Pray you, accept my humble compliments.

TRUFALDIN

Your servant.

MASCARILLE

I intrude here, I'm afraid;
But when I knew her earlier, she displayed
Great powers of divination. I hope, now, that her
Insight will help me solve a pressing matter.

TRUFALDIN

Hmm. You dabble in black magic. Is that so?

CÉLIE

My only magic is as white as snow.

MASCARILLE

Well, here's the problem. My master's heart's been captured
By a certain person; he's utterly enraptured,
And would long since have passionately expressed
To her he loves the tumult in his breast,

II

Did not a sharp-eyed dragon fiercely guard
That treasure, so that all approach is barred.
What's more, it's just now grieved him to discover
That a keen rival is enamored of her.
Therefore his heart, with anxious eagerness,
Asks if its love can hope for some success,
And I have come here, confident that you
Can give an answer sibylline and true.

CÉLIE

Under what star was he born, this master of yours?

MASCARILLE

The star of those whose truthful love endures.

CÉLIE

No need to name the maid who's won his heart;
I know her intimately, through my art.
She has much spirit, and though she must abide
An adverse fate, retains a noble pride;
She would not wish too freely to reveal
The secret stirrings that her heart may feel,
But I, who read her heart as well as she,
And am less proud, shall tell you what I see.

MASCARILLE

Oh, but the powers of magic art are great!

CÉLIE

If your master is as constant as you state,
And his intent is on the highest plane,
He need not fear that he will love in vain.
There's room for hope, and the fortress he would win
Consents to parley, and may indeed give in.

MASCARILLE
Ah, good. But this fortress has a commandant
Who's hard to handle.

CÉLIE
Yes, hard as adamant.

MASCARILLE
(Aside, looking at Lélie, who has been peering around the corner:)
The Devil take that fool, who won't stop peeking!

CÉLIE
Here's what to do, to gain the prize you're seeking.

LÉLIE
(Coming forth and joining the others.)
Don't let our visit disturb you, Trufaldin!
At my behest this faithful servingman
Has come to see you at your dwelling place
To bring my compliments, and discuss the case
Of this young lady, whose freedom I shall buy
If we can find a just price, you and I.

MASCARILLE
The idiot!

TRUFALDIN
Well, now! Someone's deceiving me!
The tales you've told me don't at all agree.

MASCARILLE
This gentleman's brain was damaged by a blow,
As you may have heard, sir.

13

TRUFALDIN

What I know, I know.
Some sneaky business is afoot, that's clear.
(*To Célie:*)
Go in. Don't leave the house again, d'you hear?
And you, you knaves, when next I'm to be tricked,
Make certain that your stories don't conflict.

(*Exit.*)

MASCARILLE

Well done! I only wish he'd given us
A well-earned thrashing for having blundered thus.
Why did you have to show yourself, and why
Did you make a speech that gave my words the lie?

LÉLIE

I thought it the thing to say.

MASCARILLE

You thought unwisely.
But why should any act of yours surprise me?
You know so many ways to botch and blunder
That no mistake of yours is grounds for wonder.

LÉLIE

Should a small slip be so fiercely reprehended?
Have I done such harm that matters can't be mended?
If you've no new scheme to make the lady mine,
Do at least thwart Léandre's sly design:
Don't let him buy Célie before I do.
Well, lest by some mistake I anger you,
I'll take my leave.

MASCARILLE

Good.

(*Exit Lélie.*)

Money, it is plain,
Would be a wondrous help in our campaign,
But having none, we'll find some other way.

Scene 5

Anselme, Mascarille.

ANSELME

It's a shameful time we live in, I must say!
Never was wealth so wastefully displayed,
Yet the loans I make are grudgingly repaid.
How blithely people borrow, yet all debts
These days are like the children one begets
In pleasure, but which cost such pain to bear.
When gold flows into our purse, we're debonair,
But when we must deliver, and get it out—
Well, that's a thing to weep and groan about.
Still, this two thousand which, for two years past,
Was owed to me, has now been paid at last.
That's something.

MASCARILLE

(*Aside:*)

　　　Look! Here comes some splendid game
To shoot at on the wing, and I shall aim
To bag him with some flattery and lies.
I well know on what theme to improvise . . .
(*To Anselme:*)
Anselme, I just saw . . .

ANSELME

Whom?

MASCARILLE

Your dear Nérine.

ANSELME

What did she say of me, that bewitching queen?

MASCARILLE

She's mad for you.

ANSELME

She is?

MASCARILLE

It pains my spirit
To see such yearning.

ANSELME

I'm gratified to hear it.

MASCARILLE

She's almost dead of love, poor little thing.
"Anselme, my dear," one hears her whimpering,
"When shall you quench these flames that you've ignited,
And our two hearts in marriage be united?"

ANSELME

But why has she hid these feelings until now?
Women are very deep, I must allow.
Tell me now, Mascarille: although I'm old,
Are my looks still fairly pleasant to behold?

MASCARILLE
Though not quite handsome, your face is very striking,
And a certain fair one finds it to her liking.

ANSELME
I see.

MASCARILLE
(Trying to seize Anselme's purse.)
        And so she's in a lovesick state,
And thinks of you as—

ANSELME
        What?

MASCARILLE
        Her future mate;
And vows to . . .

ANSELME
        What?

MASCARILLE
        To capture, come what may,
Your purse.

ANSELME
        My what?

MASCARILLE
(Taking the purse and letting it fall to the ground.)
        Your heart, I meant to say.

ANSELME

Ah yes, of course. See here, when next you see
The girl, I hope that you'll speak well of me.

MASCARILLE

Gladly.

ANSELME

Good-bye, then.

MASCARILLE

(Aside:)

Bless you! Go with God!

ANSELME

(Coming back.)
Heavens! I've just done something very odd,
And you must think me stingy, I'm afraid.
In my love affair, you've promised me your aid,
You've brought me welcome news for which I feel
Most grateful, and yet I didn't reward your zeal!
Here, so you won't forget me . . .

MASCARILLE

No, no, please!

ANSELME

Let me . . .

MASCARILLE

I don't expect gratuities.

ANSELME

I know, but still—

MASCARILLE

No, I'd be mortified;
I'm a man of honor, and it would hurt my pride.

ANSELME

Farewell, then.

MASCARILLE

(*Aside:*)
What a talker!

ANSELME

(*Coming back.*)
I've a notion to
Send the dear girl some gift by way of you;
I'll give you enough to buy her some small trinket—
A ring, perhaps, or a bracelet if you think it
Would please her taste.

MASCARILLE

No, keep your money, sir:
Leave it to me; I'll take some gift to her.
I've a charming ring that someone gave me lately,
And if it fits her, you can compensate me.

ANSELME

Good. Give it in my name, then, and endeavor
To keep her love for me as strong as ever.

Scene 6

Lélie, Anselme, Mascarille.

LÉLIE

(Picking up the purse.)
Whose purse is this?

ANSELME

I must have dropped it there!
I'd have thought a thief had taken it, I declare!
Well, thank you for the great good turn you've done me;
You've spared me much distress, and saved my money,
Which I'll take home and put away securely.

(Exit.)

MASCARILLE

You are the world's worst interferer, surely.

LÉLIE

Why, he'd have lost his purse, had I not seen it!

MASCARILLE

Oh, yes, you've done a wondrous deed! I mean it!
You've shown great timing, and vast mental powers;
Just keep it up, and victory will be ours.

LÉLIE

What have I done now?

MASCARILLE

Since you ask, I'll spell
It out. You've been a fool. F, O, O, L.
Your father will not help us, as you know;

Your rival is a formidable foe;
Yet when I try a daring ruse, and take
The risk of shame and prison for your sake . . .

LÉLIE

D'you mean? . . .

MASCARILLE

Yes, wastrel, that purse was to have been
A ransom for Célie. Then you barged in.

LÉLIE

In that case, I was wrong. But how could I guess?

MASCARILLE

It called, indeed, for rare perceptiveness!

LÉLIE

You should have given me some sign, instead—

MASCARILLE

Oh, yes, I should've had eyes in the back of my head.
Leave me alone, and in the name of Zeus,
Don't vex me with that sort of lame excuse.
After what's happened, another man would quit;
But I've just thought of a master stroke of wit,
A shrewd idea, and I shall now apply it,
So long as . . .

LÉLIE

No, I promise to keep quiet.
I'll stay away, and never interfere.

MASCARILLE

Go, then. Your presence irks me. Get out of here.

LÉLIE

For fear of Léandre, you had better hurry.

MASCARILLE

Go on, I said. I'll act at once, don't worry.
(*Exit Lélie.*)
If I can bring this off, I shall applaud
Myself as master of the art of fraud.
I'll go and . . . Good, here's just the man I'm seeking.

Scene 7

Pandolfe, Mascarille.

PANDOLFE

Mascarille!

MASCARILLE

Sir?

PANDOLFE

I'm not pleased, frankly speaking,
By the conduct of my son.

MASCARILLE

My master, sir?
You're not alone in that; I quite concur.
His bad behavior, by which I'm horrified,
Has caused my patience to be sorely tried.

PANDOLFE

That's odd. 'Twas my impression that you two
Saw eye to eye.

MASCARILLE

Ah no, sir, that's not true.
He and I always have some bone to pick;
My talk of duty makes him choleric.
Just now we quarreled, because he doesn't choose
To marry Hippolyte, and dares refuse
Your wise arrangements for him. He just won't show you
The deference which a proper son would owe you.

PANDOLFE

You quarreled?

MASCARILLE

Indeed we did; we all but fought.

PANDOLFE

Then I've been much mistaken; I always thought
That you abetted him in every way.

MASCARILLE

What! I? Well, there you have the world today,
Where innocence is wronged and misconstrued!
Sir, if you only knew my rectitude,
Though I am but his servant, I think that you
Would want to pay me as his teacher, too.
Yes, you could not more earnestly advise
Your son than I do, bidding him be wise.
Often I say to him, "In Heaven's name,
Stop drifting through this world without an aim:
Do settle down; look at the worthy sire
Whom Heaven gave you, and whom all admire;
Don't grieve him by a life of foolish whim,
But be a sound and sober man like him."

PANDOLFE

Well put. What answer does he give to that?

MASCARILLE

He fends me off with a lot of silly chat.
Mind you, I know that deep within his heart
Are the values which you've striven to impart;
But, just at present, his reason is impaired.
I could suggest a method, if I dared,
Whereby his waywardness might be restrained.

PANDOLFE

Speak on.

MASCARILLE

There's a secret which I could be caned
For uttering; but I can trust in your
Discretion, sir, and so I feel secure.

PANDOLFE

You may.

MASCARILLE

Your son resists your plans, since they've
Less charm for him than has a certain slave.

PANDOLFE

So I have heard; but now that you have said it,
The story has for me a greater credit.

MASCARILLE

I'm not your son's confederate now, you'll grant.

PANDOLFE

I grant it gladly.

MASCARILLE

Meanwhile, if you want
To lead him back to the path from which he's erred,
The way . . . I hope that I'm not overheard;
If he knew what I've been saying, he'd break my neck . . .
The way, I say, to put his plans in check
Is to purchase his belovèd captive, and
Send her in secret to some far-off land.
Anselme knows Trufaldin; dispatch him, do,
This very morning, to buy the slave for you;
Then, if you care to entrust the girl to me,
I know slave traders, and can guarantee
That you'll get back whatever she may cost,
And that all traces of her will be lost.
If your son's to settle down and wed, it's clear
That this new love of his must disappear;
For, even if he willingly complied,
And took the one you've chosen as his bride,
The nearness of this other could revive
His passion, and the marriage might not thrive.

PANDOLFE

Well said. Your plan makes sense, I'm bound to say.
Here comes Anselme; I'll seek, without delay,
To gain possession of that slave, that pest,
And put her in your hands. You'll do the rest.

MASCARILLE

(Alone:)
Good. Now to inform my master of all this.
Long live chicanery and artifice!

Scene 8

Hippolyte, Mascarille.

HIPPOLYTE

So this is how you serve me, faithless man!
Had I not overheard your crafty plan,
I'd never have believed such treachery!
You reek of falsehood, and you've lied to me.
You promised that you'd be the champion of
My hopes to wed Léandre, whom I love,
And that you'd save me in some clever way
From having to accept as fiancé
Lélie, who is my father's favorite.
Yet now you've done the very opposite!
Well, you shall not succeed, for I know how
To block the purchase you arranged just now.
I'll go . . .

MASCARILLE

My, my! You've flown right off the handle!
Your temper's flared up like a Roman candle!
Not pausing to consider that you might
Be wrong, you've hurt me by your rage and spite.
I ought to cease my services to you,
And make your unjust accusations true.

HIPPOLYTE

Would you have me doubt my senses? How absurd!
Can you deny what I just saw and heard?

MASCARILLE

No, but the whole scenario that I planned
Was in your interest, please understand.

The bill of goods that you just heard me sell
Will dupe old Pandolfe, and Anselme as well.
When by their means the captive maid is free,
I shall at once convey her to Lélie,
And it will aggravate your father so
To see how he's been hoodwinked, and to know
That his chosen son-in-law has opted out,
He'll turn then to Léandre, without a doubt.

HIPPOLYTE

What! This great scheme, which I misunderstood,
Was all for my sake?

MASCARILLE

        I sought to do you good.
But since my efforts earn no gratitude,
Since I must bear these violent shifts of mood,
And since, for all reward, you vilify me
As a base deceiver, a trickster low and slimy,
I shall reform at once, and be pure-hearted,
And put a stop to this intrigue I've started.

HIPPOLYTE

(Stopping him:)
Oh, pray don't treat me in so brusque a fashion;
Do, please, forgive my foolish burst of passion.

MASCARILLE

No, let me go. I know a way to halt
That vicious plot with which you find such fault.
You'll have no cause then to complain of me,
And you shall wed my master, wait and see.

HIPPOLYTE

Dear friend, I was an idiot to misjudge
Your good intentions; but please don't hold a grudge.
(Taking out her purse.)
Permit me, in some small way, to atone.
You wouldn't leave me helpless and alone?

MASCARILLE

No, no, I couldn't, even if I tried.
But your too hasty temper has hurt my pride.
For a man of noble mind, there's no worse wound
Than when his sacred honor has been impugned.

HIPPOLYTE

It's true, I said quite dreadful things; but please,
Let these gold Louis heal your injuries.

MASCARILLE

(Taking the coins.)
Ah, there are wrongs which gold cannot redress.
But I shall rise above all bitterness:
We must forgive our friends their little flaws.

HIPPOLYTE

Do you really think you can advance my cause
By means of this bold plot that you've devised,
And that my fond hopes may be realized?

MASCARILLE

Don't bank too much upon our present chances.
I've tricks and schemes to fit all circumstances,
And if we're luckless in my current plot,
Another will succeed where this did not.

HIPPOLYTE
Hippolyte shall be ever in your debt.

MASCARILLE
I'll serve you; but not for the gold that I may get.

HIPPOLYTE
Your master's beckoning you, and I shall go.
You'll keep on working for my cause, I know.

Scene 9

Lélie, Mascarille.

LÉLIE
Why are you idling here? You swore that you'd
Do wonders for me. Well, what ineptitude!
If my good angel hadn't warned me, I'd
Now see my hopes defeated and denied.
Farewell to joy! Farewell to happiness!
I'd be a prey to endless dark distress.
Yes, had I not been there just now, that knave
Anselme might well have bought my precious slave;
But I made such a row, and roared so well,
That Trufaldin took fright and wouldn't sell.
She's back in his house.

MASCARILLE
You've botched my plans once more!
That's three times, and I'm tired of keeping score.
I had arranged, fool, that Anselme would pay her
Ransom to Trufaldin, and then convey her
Without delay into my charge and care;

But you came meddling, and wrecked the whole affair.
Do you count on my keen wits to help you now?
No more! I'd rather I were a witless cow,
A goose, a lamppost, or a cabbage head,
And that Beelzebub would strike you dead.

LÉLIE

(Alone:)
I'd better take him to some inn that's handy,
And let him vent his fury on the brandy.

Act Two

Scene 1

Lélie, Mascarílle.

MASCARILLE

I've yielded to your pleas, although I swore
Never to serve your interests anymore,
Because I felt an itch to undertake
One final bold endeavor for your sake.
You see how pliant my heart is, and how tender;
Had Nature made me of the other gender,
Think what a passionate life I might have led!
I conjure you, however, to use your head
And not confound my present undertaking
By one of those weird blunders you've been making.
I'll beg Anselme to excuse the scene you made,
Because our new plot will require his aid;

But one more gaffe, and I shall cease to care
Whether you prosper in your love affair.

LÉLIE

No, no, you needn't worry, I promise you.
I'll watch my step.

MASCARILLE

Make certain that you do.
Now, I've devised for you a daring scheme.
Your father has been slow in the extreme
To die, and leave you with the funds you need,
And so I've killed him—in word, if not in deed.
I've spread a rumor about him, telling folk
That the old boy's had a sudden, fatal stroke.
But first, to give that lie an honest face,
I made him vanish to his country place.
I sent a man to tell him that the crew
Of workmen he'd engaged to dig a new
Foundation for his barn had just now found
A chest of treasure buried in the ground.
Well! Off to the country, in a flash, he flew,
With all his household, save for me and you,
And I could now announce his death, you see,
And promptly bury him in effigy.
There now: You have the outline of our plot.
Play your part carefully, and if I do not
Follow the script, or if I miss my cues,
Call me an ass, or any name you choose.

LÉLIE

(Alone:)
He's found a very strange and devious way
To make my dreams come true, I'm bound to say.

But when a girl has set one's heart on fire,
What won't one do to gain the heart's desire?
Passion, which is considered to excuse
Great crimes, should justify this little ruse,
To which my love and my envisagement
Of future joys have forced me to consent.
Good heavens; listen! Our play's about to start;
I must get in the mood to play my part.

Scene 2

Anselme, Mascarílle.

MASCARILLE

You're taken aback, I know, by news so grim.

ANSELME

What a way to die!

MASCARILLE

'Twas very wrong of him
To play us such a sudden, shocking trick.

ANSELME

He didn't even take time to be sick!

MASCARILLE

No man was ever in such haste to die.

ANSELME

How is Lélie?

MASCARILLE

Alas, he's maddened by
His grief; he beats his breast; I hear him rave
That he wants to follow his papa to the grave.
Indeed, his anguish causes me such worry
That I've had the corpse enshrouded in a hurry,
For fear that its depressing sight could lead
The poor boy to commit some fatal deed.

ANSELME

Still, you should have waited longer. —I'd have preferred
To see him again before he was interred.
It can be murder to bury a man too quickly;
Many a man looks dead when he's just sickly.

MASCARILLE

I assure you that, in the fullest sense, he's dead.
But, to return to what we earlier said,
Lélie's conceived a loving son's desire
To hold a lavish funeral for his sire,
And thus, through rites and honors, give at least
Some consolation to the dear deceased.
He has a fine inheritance, but he's
A babe in business, and thus far all he sees
Are funds tied up in distant tracts of land
And bonds he can't convert to cash in hand.
Therefore he begs you, if you can forget
His recent conduct, which fills him with regret,
To lend him what the obsequies will cost . . .

ANSELME

Yes. First, I'll go see the dear friend I have lost.

(Exit.)

MASCARILLE

(Alone:)
Our plot is launched, and goes ahead full sail;
Let's stay alert now, or our hopes may fail.
Lest, in the very port, we come to grief,
Let's steer with care 'round every rock and reef.

Scene 3

Anselme, Lélie, Mascarille.

ANSELME

Alas, it pains me more than I can say
To see him wrapped up in that mournful way.
He was just alive, and now he's dead. How strange!

MASCARILLE

In a short time, a man can greatly change.

LÉLIE

(Weeping:)
Ohh!

ANSELME

He was but mortal. Even Rome, my dear Lélie,
Cannot dispense us from mortality.

LÉLIE

Ohh!

ANSELME

Death, without warning, claims all humankind.
All through our lives it stalks us, close behind.

LÉLIE

Ohh!

ANSELME

Deaf to all our prayers, that ravenous beast
Will not forgo one morsel of his feast;
He eats us all.

LÉLIE

Ohh!

MASCARILLE

Your preaching is in vain;
It can't eradicate so deep a pain.

ANSELME

If my words, Lélie, can't heal this bitter blow,
Do try, at least, to moderate your woe.

LÉLIE

Ohh!

MASCARILLE

To curb his grief just now is out of the question.

ANSELME

In any case, at your valet's suggestion,
I've brought a sum of money which should with ease
Pay for your worthy father's obsequies.

LÉLIE

Ohh! Ohh!

MASCARILLE

How that word "father" makes him cry!
At the thought of what he's lost, he longs to die.

ANSELME

When you check the dear man's books, you'll notice there
That I owe much more than this to you, his heir;
But even if I owed you nothing at all,
My fortune would be at your beck and call.
Take this; whatever I possess is yours.

LÉLIE

(Going.)
Ohh!

MASCARILLE

My poor master. What anguish he endures!

ANSELME

Mascarille, I think that it would be discreet
For him to dash me off a short receipt.

MASCARILLE

Ohh!

ANSELME

There are always unforeseen events.

MASCARILLE

Ohh!

ANSELME

Just the briefest of acknowledgments.

MASCARILLE

Ah, how can he write things in his present state?
Permit this stormy sorrow to abate,
And once his woes have given him some rest,
I'll have him sign the paper you request.
Farewell. My heart is bursting. I shall go
To my master's side, and let my salt tears flow.
Ohh!

ANSELME

(Alone:)

    In this troubled world, no man can keep
From meeting daily with some cause to weep.
Yes, here below . . .

Scene 4

Pandolfe, Anselme.

ANSELME

    Oh, God! What's this? Alack,
Pandolfe won't rest in peace; he's coming back!
Now that he's dead, how pale his cheeks appear!
No! Keep your distance! Kindly don't come near!
I just don't care to touch a man who's dead.

PANDOLFE

What is this nonsense? Are you off your head?

ANSELME

Why are you here? Stand back, and tell me why.
If you're looking for me so as to say good-bye,
You're being much too formal. Believe you me,

I could have done without this courtesy.
If your soul's in torment and in need of prayers,
I'll tend to that, but let's have no more scares!
On the word of a terrified man, I'll go full speed
To the church, and buy you all the prayers you need.
(*He kneels.*)

Ghost, ghost, go away!
So upon my knees I pray.
May your spirit be at rest,
And in Heaven be ever blest.

PANDOLFE

(*Laughing:*)
I don't know whether to laugh, or be offended.

ANSELME

You're very gay for a man whose life has ended!

PANDOLFE

Is this a joke, or have your brains decayed?
Why treat a living person as a shade?

ANSELME

I've seen your corpse. You're dead; I cannot doubt it.

PANDOLFE

What! Can a man die, and not know about it?

ANSELME

Alas, when Mascarille first let me know
The tragic news, I almost died of woe.

PANDOLFE

Enough, now. If you're asleep, it's time to waken.
Do you not see me in the flesh?

ANSELME

You've taken
A spectral form that's not unlike your own,
But which, in a trice, could change to shapes unknown.
I tremble lest you swell to giant size,
With a huge, ugly face and burning eyes.
For God's sake, don't become some hideous freak,
Or I shall be too horrified to speak.

PANDOLFE

At another time, Anselme, the naïveté
And droll credulity that you display
Would give me much to jest and chaff about,
And I might wish to draw the subject out:
But this reported death of mine, combined
With a fake treasure I was sent to find,
Appear to justify my strong belief
That Mascarille's a villain, knave and thief
Who has no fear or conscience, and descends
To the basest trickery to gain his ends.

ANSELME

Have I been hoodwinked? Am I a dupe, a clown?
Oh, my intelligence, how you've let me down!
Just to be sure, I'll touch him; yes, it's he.
Plague take the ass that I've turned out to be!
Don't spread this story abroad, in Heaven's name;
They'd write a farce about me; I'd die of shame.
But now, Pandolfe, I hope you'll help me to
Get back the money I lent to bury you.

PANDOLFE

Money, you say? Ah, that's the answer! There
Is the hidden motive in this whole affair:
Well, that's your worry. I'll go complain of these
Dishonest actions to the authorities,
And once they catch that Mascarille, I'll hope
To see him dangle from a hangman's rope.

ANSELME

(Alone:)
I've been a credulous fool, a trusting dunce,
And lost my cunning and my cash at once.
Gray hair becomes me, if I now can make
This sort of senile, doddering mistake,
And fall so readily into a snare.
But look . . .

Scene 5

Lélie, Anselme.

LÉLIE

(Not seeing Anselme.)
        Now, with this passport that I bear,
I know that Trufaldin will welcome me.

ANSELME

Your sorrow has left you, I am glad to see.

LÉLIE

What's that? Oh, no, sir. Woe shall never leave
This orphaned heart, which must forever grieve.

ANSELME

I hurried back to tell you that, by chance,
That purse could cause you trouble. Though at a glance
The coins look good, I fear that I mixed in,
By error, a few which are not genuine,
And I've brought honest gold to exchange for those.
Alas, these counterfeiters! Their number grows
Each year, and thanks to them it's come about
That all transactions now are tinged with doubt.
Hang all such rascals! They deserve to die.

LÉLIE

You're kind to replace the bogus coins, though I
Did not see any. They must be hard to spot.

ANSELME

I'll recognize them; here, let me have the lot.
It's all here?

LÉLIE

Yes.

ANSELME

        Good. Now, you're mine once more,
Dear purse. Slip into my pocket, as before.
Young thief, you'll get no more ill-gotten wealth.
So, you bury a man when he's in perfect health!
To a poor old father-in-law, what might you have done?
To think I'd chosen you to be my son,
And wanted Hippolyte to take your name!
Be off. Go die, sir, of remorse and shame.

LÉLIE

(*Alone:*)
Well, he saw through me. But how could he be so quick
To grow suspicious of our clever trick?

Scene 6

Lélie, Mascarille.

MASCARILLE

So, you'd gone out! I've looked for you everywhere.
Well, now! Success at last! I do declare
That I've no equal as a scheming knave.
Give me the money, and I'll go buy our slave.
Your rival's going to be thunderstruck.

LÉLIE

Ah, my dear fellow, I fear we're out of luck.
You won't believe the bitterness of my lot.

MASCARILLE

What are you saying?

LÉLIE

Anselme divined our plot,
And, offering to replace some counterfeit
Coins in that purse, he just made off with it.

MASCARILLE

You're joking, surely?

LÉLIE

I fear it's all too true.

MASCARILLE

You really mean it?

LÉLIE

Unfortunately, I do.
And now, I know, you're going to be furious.

MASCARILLE

I, sir? Of course not. Anger is injurious
To health, and I let nothing trouble me.
Whether Célie's in bondage or goes free,
Whether Léandre buys her, or does not,
Are matters I don't care about one jot.

LÉLIE

Oh, don't deny me your concern and aid,
And please forgive the little slip I made!
Up to that time, you'll grant, I'd played the part
Of a grief-stricken son with wondrous art;
The sharpest eye could never have perceived
That I was not most horribly bereaved.

MASCARILLE

Go on and praise yourself I couldn't care less.

LÉLIE

Oh, well. I made a mess of it, I confess.
But if you wish me happy, I hope you will
Forget my stupid error, and help me still.

MASCARILLE

Your servant, sir. I've other things to do.

LÉLIE

Dear Mascarille!

MASCARILLE

No.

LÉLIE

Help me, I beg of you.

MASCARILLE

No, I'll do nothing.

LÉLIE

If you won't change your mind,
I'll kill myself.

MASCARILLE

Do, if you're so inclined.

LÉLIE

You won't relent?

MASCARILLE

No.

LÉLIE

You see that my sword is drawn?

MASCARILLE

Yes.

LÉLIE

I shall thrust it through my heart.

MASCARILLE

Go on.

LÉLIE

Won't you be sad to have taken my life from me?

MASCARILLE

No.

LÉLIE

Then, farewell.

MASCARILLE

Farewell, Monsieur Lélie.

LÉLIE

So! . . .

MASCARILLE

Hurry up, please; less talk, more suicide.

LÉLIE

Because you'd get my wardrobe if I died,
You'd have me play the fool and pierce my heart.

MASCARILLE

I knew that you were faking, from the start.
Men often swear to kill themselves, and yet
Few of them, nowadays, make good their threat.

Scene 7

Trufaldin, Léandre, Lélie, Mascarille. Trufaldin and Léandre confer in low voices at stage rear.

LÉLIE

Look! Léandre and Trufaldin in conversation!
He'll buy Célie! Oh, dread and trepidation!

MASCARILLE

No doubt he wants to buy her, and if he's got
Money enough, he'll get her, like as not.
Well, I'm delighted: It's the price that must be paid
For all the blundering rashness you've displayed.

LÉLIE

What can I do now, in this fearful plight?

MASCARILLE

Who knows?

LÉLIE

I know; I'll challenge him to a fight.

MASCARILLE

What good would come of that?

LÉLIE

Advise me, then:
How can I stop him?

MASCARILLE

There, there; I'll once again
Show pity and forgive you. Leave me now;

I'll keep an eye upon him, and learn somehow,
By peaceful means, how his affairs proceed.

(*Exit Lélie.*)

TRUFALDIN

(*To Leandre:*)
When the man comes, I'll deliver, as agreed.

(*Exit Trufaldin.*)

MASCARILLE

(*Aside, as he exits:*)
I must deceive him, so that he'll unveil
His plans to me, and I can make them fail.

LÉANDRE

(*Alone:*)
    Thank Heaven, my happiness is guaranteed;
What I've arranged is certain to succeed.
There's nothing now to fear, and I'm exempt
From anything my rival might attempt.

MASCARILLE

(*Utters these two lines offstage, then enters:*)
Ouch! Ouch! Help, murder! Oh, what a cruel blow!
Stop it, you brute, you monster! Oh! Oh! Oh!

LÉANDRE

What's this? What ails you? Why these cries of pain?

MASCARILLE

Two hundred blows he gave me, with his cane.

LÉANDRE

Who did?

MASCARILLE

Lélie.

LÉANDRE

But why?

MASCARILLE

For a mere bagatelle
He's thrown me out, and beaten me as well.

LÉANDRE

That's very wrong of him.

MASCARILLE

As soon as I can,
I vow to avenge myself on that vile man.
Yes, you shall learn, you brute who've battered me,
That you can't strike me with impunity,
That, servant though I am, I have my pride,
And that my four years' service at your side
Did not deserve this harsh emolument,
Which both my honor and my back resent.
Yes, I shall be avenged! You've wished me to
Secure a certain charming slave for you,
But I'll make sure now that some other lover,
With my assistance, will deprive you of her.

LÉANDRE

Do calm your anger, Mascarille, and hear me.
I've always liked you, and have wished sincerely
That a keen, loyal fellow of your kind

Might some day be my servant. If you're inclined
To accept the post I offer, and serve me in it,
I'll take you into my employ this minute.

                    MASCARILLE
Sir, I accept your offer with delight,
Because, in serving you, I'll serve him right,
And shall, in my endeavors for your sake,
Punish the beast whose cane has made me ache.
I'm sure that, through my artful aid, Célie . . .

                    LÉANDRE
That goal's already been achieved, by me.
Charmed by that girl, who has no peer on earth,
I've just now bought her, for far less than she's worth.

                    MASCARILLE
Célie is yours, then?

                    LÉANDRE
            You'd see her here beside me
If I had only my desires to guide me:
But Father rules my life; he lately sent
Me word that it's his wish and firm intent
That I wed Hippolyte. He'd rage, I fear,
If rumors of Célie should reach his ear.
With Trufaldin, I thought it best to claim
That I was acting in another's name;
And we agreed that he was to consign
Célie to a man who'd show this ring of mine.
But first I must devise a means whereby
To hide my charmer from the public eye,
And find for her some quiet place where she
Can dwell in comfort and in secrecy.

MASCARILLE

Not far from town, I've an old kinsman whose
Small house I could arrange for you to use.
It's most secluded; no one would be aware
That you had secretly installed her there.

LÉANDRE

You've solved my problem; it sounds like just the thing.
Go, then, to Trufaldin, and take this ring.
As soon as he sees it, he'll release the fair
Captive whom I adore into your care.
And you can take her then to that retreat
Of which you speak. But hush! Here's Hippolyte.

Scene 8

Hippolyte, Léandre, Mascarille.

HIPPOLYTE

I have some news for you, Léandre—though
Whether you'll like or loathe it, I don't know.

LÉANDRE

Before I tell you what my feelings are,
I'll have to hear it.

HIPPOLYTE

Then walk with me as far
As the church, and I shall tell you on the way.

LÉANDRE

(To Mascarille:)
Go, do me that small service. And hurry, pray.

MASCARILLE

(*Alone:*)
I'll serve you, sir, with a dish of humble pie.
What rascal could be luckier than I?
What joy Lélie will shortly feel! What bliss
That the girl should drop into our hands like this!
How fine that a rival, bent on our defeat,
Has handed us a victory so sweet!
After this triumph, they'll paint me with a wreath
On my heroic brow, and underneath
Will be the glorious title I've always sought for:
MASCARILLUS RASCALUM IMPERATOR.

Scene 9

Trufaldin, Mascarille.

MASCARILLE

Ho, there!

TRUFALDIN

(*Opening his door.*)
    What do you want?

MASCARILLE

    It should be clear,
From this familiar ring, what brings me here.

TRUFALDIN

I know the ring, and I know your errand, too.
Wait here a moment; I'll fetch the slave for you.

Scene 10

Trufaldin, a Messenger, Mascarille.

MESSENGER

(To Trufaldin:)
Sir, be so kind as to tell me where a man . . .

TRUFALDIN

What man?

MESSENGER

I think his name is Trufaldin.

TRUFALDIN

You're looking at him. What do you want him for?

MESSENGER

To put this letter in his hand, no more.

TRUFALDIN

(Reading:)

The kindness of that Heaven which we adore
Has lately brought the welcome news to me
That my daughter, kidnapped at the age of four,
Is now your slave, and bears the name "Célie."
If you have been a father, and have known
How deep and tender is that natural bond,
Then pray protect, as if she were your own,
The precious child of whom I am so fond.
I shall set out at once to repossess
My daughter, and give you a reward so fine,
So opulent, that in your happiness

You'll bless the day when you returned me mine.
Don Pedro De Gusman,
Marquis of Montalcana,
Madrid.

(Trufaldin continues, aside:)
Gypsies are not renowned for speaking truly,
Yet those who brought Célie and sold her to me
Said that a rich man soon would pay her ransom,
And that the payment would be more than handsome.
Great heavens! In my doubt and my impatience,
I almost lost my golden expectations.
(To the Messenger:)
Your message got here with no time to spare:
I'd all but given her to that fellow there.
But now I'll keep her safe, in every way.
(Exit the Messenger. To Mascarille:)
You've heard, of course, what the letter had to say.
Go tell the man who sent you here that I
Can't keep our bargain. Ask him to come by
And get his money back.

MASCARILLE
                    Sir, he'll be nettled
By such a breach of—

TRUFALDIN
Go, the matter's settled.

MASCARILLE
(Alone:)
That blasted letter was bad news for us,
And fortune has indeed been treacherous!
At a fatal moment, that rogue arrived from Spain;

May he go back through thunder, hail and rain!
Never has such a fine beginning had
An ending quite so sudden or so sad.

Scene 11

Lélie (laughing), Mascarille.

MASCARILLE

Well, well. What is it that delights you so?

LÉLIE

When I've finished laughing, I shall let you know.

MASCARILLE

Laugh, by all means; it's just the time for laughter.

LÉLIE

You'll never again complain of me; hereafter,
You won't be able to scold me as the man
Whose bungling spoils your every plot and plan,
For I've just played a shrewd trick of my own.
I can be rash and hasty, as I've shown,
But when I'm in the mood I can contrive
Fine schemes as well as any man alive,
And you yourself will grant that what I've done
Displays a wit unmatched by anyone.

MASCARILLE

Well, what have you done? Don't keep me in suspense.

LÉLIE

Just now, when I saw my foe in conference
With Trufaldin, I felt a deep disquiet,

And, seeking for some way to rectify it,
Marshaled my powers and, by means of them,
Conceived and carried out a stratagem
Which, if compared to the dazzling tricks you've played,
Is brighter still, and puts them in the shade.

MASCARILLE

Exactly what? . . .

LÉLIE

Be patient, please. I wrote
And sent to Trufaldin a spurious note,
Signed by a nobleman of my invention,
Who said that Heaven had brought to his attention
The fact that his lost daughter, now called "Célie,"
Was dwelling, as a slave, with the addressee.
He conjured Trufaldin to give good care
To the girl, until her father could be there,
Adding that he was leaving Spain that day
And planned upon arrival to repay
The latter's kindness with a lavish sum.

MASCARILLE

Splendid.

LÉLIE

But wait, the best is yet to come.
The messenger who gave Trufaldin my letter
Said that its timing couldn't have been better!
A man had claimed Célie, and was about
To bear her off, but the fool was put to rout.

MASCARILLE

Did the Devil help you in this bright endeavor?

LÉLIE

Would you have dreamt that I could be so clever?
You should commend the style and expertise
With which I foiled my rival's strategies.

MASCARILLE

I fear I lack the eloquence and strength
To praise your deed with proper force and length.
My tongue is powerless to describe the bold
Exploit which I was privileged to behold,
And the workings of a wit which can "contrive
Fine schemes as well as any man alive."
I wish, indeed, that I possessed a mind
In which all art and wisdom were combined,
And so could tell you in great prose or verse
That you will always be, for better or worse,
What you have been from the hour of your birth—
That is to say, the rashest fool on earth,
A man whose reason is deranged and ill,
Whose judgment's warped, whose common sense is nil,
A blunderer, a dolt, a knucklehead,
And . . . a hundred other things I might have said.
There's a brief sample of the praise that's due you.

LÉLIE

Have I done something that's annoying to you?
Why are you angry? What can the reason be?

MASCARILLE

No, you've done nothing; but don't you follow me.

LÉLIE

I'll follow you until I get an answer.

MASCARILLE

Will you? Then run as quickly as you can, sir.
I'll give your legs a bit of exercise.

LÉLIE

(*Alone:*)
He's got away. Alas, I can't surmise
The reason for that violent tirade.
What blunder can I possibly have made?

Act Three

Scene 1

Mascarille.

MASCARILLE

Hush, my good nature; you haven't a grain of sense,
And I'll no longer hear your arguments.
It's you, my anger, that I'll listen to.
Am I obliged forever to undo
The blunders of a clod? I should resign!
That fool has spoiled too many schemes of mine.
And yet, let's think about this matter coolly.
Were I to let my just impatience rule me,
They'd say that I'd been quick to call it quits,
And that I'd lost the vigor of my wits;
And what then would become of my renown
As the most glorious trickster in the town,
A reputation that I've earned by never

Failing to think of something wildly clever?
O Mascarille, let honor be your guide!
Persist in those great works which are your pride,
And though your master irks you, persevere
Not for his sake, but for your own career.
Yet what can you accomplish, when the force
Of a demonic head wind blocks your course,
And you're compelled to tack and tack again?
What is the use of persevering, when
His folly brings continual heavy weather,
And sinks the best schemes you can put together?
Well, out of kindness, let us give it one
Final attempt, and see what can be done;
Then, if he wrecks our chances as before,
I swear that I'll not help him anymore.
We might, in fact, accomplish our desire
If we could get our rival to retire—
If, backing off, Léandre would allow
Me one whole day for the plot I'm hatching now.
Yes, I'm now thinking out an artful plan
Which surely will succeed, if I but can
Remove the obstacle I've spoken of
He's coming: I'll test the firmness of his love.

Scene 2

Léandre, Mascarille.

MASCARILLE

Bad news, sir; Trufaldin won't keep his word.

LÉANDRE

I've just now seen him, and that's what I heard.
I've also learned that that romantic blather

About a stolen child whose noble father
Is coming with a bag of gold from Spain
Is purest fabrication and chicane,
Whereby Lélie has kept, for a day or two,
My purchase of Célie from going through.

MASCARILLE

What a beast he is!

LÉANDRE

Yet Trufaldin's unable
To see that story as a silly fable,
And has so greedily swallowed all those lies
That no one can persuade him otherwise.

MASCARILLE

He'll keep her now in strictest custody;
There's nothing we can do, that I can see.

LÉANDRE

From the very first, I felt affection for her,
But now, in truth, I utterly adore her,
And there are many times when I incline
To drop all caution and to make her mine—
To change her bonds for those of wedded life,
And mend her lot by making her my wife.

MASCARILLE

You'd marry her?

LÉANDRE

Well, I'm not entirely sure;
But though her background is a bit obscure,
Her grace and virtue have, it must be said,
A power to win one's heart and turn one's head.

MASCARILLE

Her virtue? Hmm.

LÉANDRE

What? Why do you grunt when I
Make mention of her virtue? Tell me why.

MASCARILLE

Your countenance, sir, is darker than before;
I would be wise, perhaps, to say no more.

LÉANDRE

No, no, speak out.

MASCARILLE

Well then, from Christian kindness,
I shall proceed to cure you of your blindness.
That wench . . .

LÉANDRE

Go on.

MASCARILLE

Is anything but chilly.
In secret, she's a most obliging filly,
And any man who treats her well will find
That her heart isn't of the flinty kind.
She seems demure, and feigns to be a prude,
But I can speak of her with certitude.
It's part of my profession, you might say,
To know the shady games that people play.

LÉANDRE

But—

MASCARILLE

Her modesty's the purest of pretenses;
Her virtue is a fort without defenses,
A shadow which, as many a man could tell,
The glitter of a gold piece can dispel.

LÉANDRE

What are you saying? How can I believe . . .

MASCARILLE

Do as you like, sir; you're free to be naive.
Yes, doubt my word and do as you have planned—
Purchase the wench, and offer her your hand.
The whole town will applaud you, for you'll be
The keeper of its common property.

LÉANDRE

I'm stunned.

MASCARILLE

(Aside:)
        Aha! This fish begins to bite,
And if I hook him well, and play him right,
We shall have one impediment the less.

LÉANDRE

I'm overcome with horror and distress.

MASCARILLE

Well, now you . . .

LÉANDRE

Go to the post house, please, and see
If there's a letter there addressed to me.

(*Alone, having brooded for a moment or two:*)
It's true, no doubt; but how was one to tell?
Never did any face deceive so well.

Scene 3

Lélie, Léandre.

LÉLIE

Why is it that you look so very sad?

LÉANDRE

I?

LÉLIE

You.

LÉANDRE

I have no grounds for feeling bad.

LÉLIE

Oh, yes, you do: Célie is on your mind.

LÉANDRE

My thoughts don't stoop to trifles of that kind.

LÉLIE

You had great plans for snaring her somehow,
But since they failed, you feign indifference now.

LÉANDRE

If I were fool enough to pin my dreams
On her, I'd soon make mock of all your schemes.

LÉLIE

What schemes?

LÉANDRE

Come, come! We know it all, my friend.

LÉLIE

All what?

LÉANDRE

Your whole campaign, from end to end.

LÉLIE

What can you mean? You're talking gibberish.

LÉANDRE

Claim not to understand me, if you wish.
But let me tell you something: You needn't fear
That I'll try to take away your captive dear.
I worship beauty when it's fresh and chaste,
But I can't yearn for what has been debased.

LÉLIE

Take care, Léandre!

LÉANDRE

Oh, how you've been taken in!
Go on, then; court this spotless heroine,
And boast then of your amorous success.
She has uncommon beauty, I confess,
But the rest of her, Lélie, is common stuff

LÉLIE

No more such talk, Léandre; that's enough.
Vie with me all you like, and strive to claim her,

But let's not hear you slander and defame her.
I charge myself with utter cowardice
For letting you blaspheme Célie like this,
And though I can endure it that you love her,
I cannot brook your speaking evil of her.

LÉANDRE

I've good authority for speaking so.

LÉLIE

Whoever said such things is false and low.
The girl is wholly innocent and pure;
I know her heart.

LÉANDRE

But Mascarille, I'm sure,
Is a good judge of hearts and their affairs,
And he condemns her.

LÉLIE

He?

LÉANDRE

Yes, he.

LÉLIE

He dares
Malign a blameless girl, who lives uprightly?
Does he suppose that I will take that lightly?
He'll eat his words!

LÉANDRE

I wager he will not.

LÉLIE

By God, I'd beat him senseless on the spot,
If he dared reiterate so base a lie.

LÉANDRE

I'd crop his ears if he were to deny
The things he told me. He'd better stand his ground.

Scene 4

Lélie, Léandre, Mascarille.

LÉLIE

Ah, there he is! Come here, you cursèd hound.

MASCARILLE

What?

LÉLIE

Yes, you monster of duplicity,
How could you sink your fangs into Célie,
Blackening the virtue of the brightest maid
Ever to dwell within misfortune's shade?

MASCARILLE

(*Sotto voce, to Lélie:*)
Calm down, sir; it's just part of a little hoax.

LÉLIE

No, none of your winking; none of your merry jokes;
I'm blind and deaf to all you do and say.
Were you my brother, there'd still be Hell to pay,
For anyone who speaks a calumny

Of her I love has deeply wounded me.
Stop making faces! Now, what did you say, you scum?

MASCARILLE

I'm going, sir, lest our talk grow quarrelsome.

LÉLIE

No, you shall stay.

MASCARILLE

Ouch!

LÉLIE

Out with it, now! Confess.

MASCARILLE

(Sotto voce, to Lélie:)
'Twas just a bit of intrigue—no more, no less.

LÉLIE

Enough, now. Tell me, what did you say of her?

MASCARILLE

(Sotto voce, to Lélie:)
I said what I said; don't lose your temper, sir.

LÉLIE

(Drawing his sword.)
You'll change your tune, by Heaven, before I'm through!

LÉANDRE

(Stopping him.)
Don't let your anger run away with you.

MASCARILLE

(Aside:)
In all the world, was there ever a brain so dim?

LÉLIE

Come, let me wreak my righteous wrath on him.

LÉANDRE

If you struck him in my presence, I'd take offense.

LÉLIE

Can't I punish my own servant? That makes no sense.

LÉANDRE

Your servant?

MASCARILLE

(Aside:)
Ohh! He'll soon see through my plot.

LÉLIE

If I want to beat him to death, why should I not?
He is, after all, my man.

LÉANDRE

He's my man now.

LÉLIE

That's most amusing. Kindly tell me how
He comes to be yours.

MASCARILLE

(Sotto voce, to Lélie:)
Take care.

LÉLIE

What's that you say?

MASCARILLE

(Aside:)
What a dolt! He's bound to give the game away.
He sees my signals, but he pays no heed.

LÉLIE

Léandre, you have strange ideas indeed.
He's not my man, eh?

LÉANDRE

Wasn't he shown the door
Because of some small thing you blamed him for?

LÉLIE

That's news to me.

LÉANDRE

And didn't you bestow
A savage beating when you bade him go?

LÉLIE

What! I discharge my man? And thrash him too?
You're having fun with me . . . or he with you.

MASCARILLE

(Aside:)
Go on, fool: You're your own worst adversary.

LÉANDRE

(To Mascarille:)
So, that fierce beating was imaginary!

MASCARILLE

It's slipped his mind. His memory's—

LÉANDRE

No, no,
As all the evidence now seems to show,
You've played me a crafty trick, which I'll forgive
Because the ruse was so imaginative.
It's enough for me that I now know the facts,
And know the motive for your cunning acts,
And that, considering how hard I fell
For your deceits, I've come off pretty well.
Henceforth I'll be more cautious, thanks to you.
Your humble servant, dear Lélie. Adieu.

(Exit Léandre.)

MASCARILLE

Courage, my boy; our cause must never yield.
Let's draw our swords and bravely take the field;
We'll sweep to victory like Huns or Vandals!

LÉLIE

He said that you were spreading filthy scandals
About . . .

MASCARILLE

Why wouldn't you go along with my
Deceptions, which he'd swallowed, and whereby
I'd all but killed his feelings for Célie?
But no, my master wouldn't lie, not he!
I win his rival's confidence, and the dunce
Gives me a chance to steal Célie at once;
My master ruins everything, however,

By a note from Spain which frustrates my endeavor.
I undermine his rival's passion, but then
My master comes and props it up again,
Ignores my winks and whispers, and refuses
To stop till he's dismantled all my ruses.
Rare work by one who says he can "contrive
Fine schemes as well as any man alive"!
Such art as you have shown should hang, say I,
In the king's gorgeous palace at Versailles.

LÉLIE

It isn't *my* fault that I sometimes mar
Your plans; if you don't tell me what they are,
I'm bound to do so.

MASCARILLE

So much the worse for you.

LÉLIE

You'd have a right to chide me if I knew
A bit about the plots you were devising;
But since you tell me nothing, it's not surprising
That I am made to seem a blundering fool.

MASCARILLE

You really ought to run a fencing school.
How well you avoid the point! And your deflection
Of my attack is something like perfection.

LÉLIE

What's done is done; let's let the subject drop.
My rival, in any case, can't put a stop
To our endeavors, and I rely on you . . .

MASCARILLE

If you don't mind, let's drop that subject, too.
My anger's not so easily mollified,
And if you want my temper to subside,
You must do me a service first. I'll ponder then
Whether to run your love campaigns again.

LÉLIE

Whatever you ask, I'll happily accord.
Do you need my good right arm, my trusty sword?

MASCARILLE

What brutal fancies occupy his mind!
You sound like some swashbuckler of the kind
That's always readier to draw a blade
Than draw his purse and give a poor man aid.

LÉLIE

What, then, can I do for you?

MASCARILLE

Go see your sire;
Do everything you can to appease his ire.

LÉLIE

I've gained his pardon.

MASCARILLE

Well, I have not. I spread
A rumor, for your sake, that he was dead,
And it upset him greatly. One gets no thanks
From agèd men for playing them such pranks,
And causing them to contemplate with fear
The melancholy end that's drawing near.

The old boy's still in love with life, and he
Sees nothing funny in mortality;
He's furious and, according to report,
It's his intent to haul me into court.
I fear that, if I took up residence
In prison, living at the king's expense,
It might be long before I was at large.
I've been accused of many an unjust charge,
For virtue's hated in these wicked times,
And persecuted like the worst of crimes.
Go. Make him forgive me.

LÉLIE

I'll do so; count on me.
But promise me in return . . .

MASCARILLE

Yes, yes. We'll see.
(*Exit Lélie.*)
Now I'll relax, and yield to my fatigue.
No plots for a while, no dodges, no intrigue,
No more behaving like a man possessed.
Léandre can't act against our interest,
Because Célie is under lock and key . . .

Scene 5

Ergaste, Mascarille.

ERGASTE

Ah! I've been looking for you, Mascarille.
There's a secret matter of which I've just got word.

MASCARILLE

What is it, Ergaste?

ERGASTE

We won't be overheard?

MASCARILLE

No.

ERGASTE

As your bosom friend, I'm well aware
Of the part you play in your master's love affair.
Well, be on your guard. Léandre has a plan
To steal Célie away from Trufaldin
This very night. He, having understood
That certain ladies of the neighborhood
Go visiting in masks this time of year,
Has planned his own sly masquerade, I hear.

MASCARILLE

Is that so? Well, he's not yet won the day.
I just might fool him, and rob him of his prey.
Yes, I'll turn his tricks against him! It won't be hard
To hoist the fellow with his own petard.
He doesn't know my gifts, Ergaste. Adieu;
When next we meet, we'll drain a glass or two.
(*Exit Ergaste.*)
I'll borrow our rival's plan, converting it
Adroitly to my master's benefit,
And thus, by a maneuver bold yet wise,
Avoid all risk, yet carry off the prize.
If I don a mask, and get there first, then I'll
Be sure at least to cramp Léandre's style;
And if I manage to achieve our aim

And steal Célie, it's he who'll get the blame!
Since word of his scheme's already gotten out,
It's he who'd be accused, beyond a doubt,
And so I undertake this dangerous mission
Without a qualm, and fearless of suspicion.
This is called being subtle, shrewd and cool,
And using someone as a pawn, or tool.
Well, I must hurry and enlist the aid
Of a few comrades for this masquerade;
I have connections, and I can supply
Both men and gear in the twinkling of an eye.
'Twill be a brilliant coup, believe you me;
The Lord endowed me with rascality,
And I am not the thankless sort of knave
Who hides beneath a bushel what Heaven gave.

Scene 6

Lélie, Ergaste.

LÉLIE

So, he'll gain entry as a masquer, then,
And carry her off?

ERGASTE
Exactly. One of his men
Told me as much, and I ran instantly
To break the whole affair to Mascarille,
Who left at once to foil Léandre's plot
By some device he'd thought of on the spot.
Soon afterward, I met by chance with you,
And thought it best, sir, to inform you, too.

LÉLIE

For this intelligence, I'm in your debt.
Go. What you've done for me, I shan't forget.
(Exit Ergaste.)
My knave will play them some fine trick, I know;
But I'm moved to help him, and somehow strike a blow.
It's wrong, in matters which concern me most,
That I should stand by like a stump or post.
Night's falling. They'll be surprised to see me there.
I should have brought my musket, I declare.
But let who will attack me! By the Lord,
I've two good pistols and a good sharp sword.
Ho there, inside!

Scene 7

Trufaldin (at his window), Lélie.

TRUFALDIN

Who called me, and what for?

LÉLIE

Make sure, this evening, that you've locked the door.

TRUFALDIN

Why?

LÉLIE

There's a merry troupe of masquers coming,
Who mean to treat you to some curious mumming;
They plan to abduct Célie.

TRUFALDIN

They do? Oh, dear!

LÉLIE

I have no doubt that they will soon be here.
Stay at your window, and you'll see the show.
There now, they're coming! Didn't I tell you so?
Hush! I'll confront them, and we'll have some fun
With these impostors, unless they cut and run.

Scene 8

Lélie, Trufaldin, Mascarille and his company (masked and in dresses).

TRUFALDIN

Rogues! It takes more to fool me than a mask!

LÉLIE

Well, ladies! Where are you off to, may I ask?
Let them in, Trufaldin; they'll dance and sing.
(To Mascarille, disguised as a woman:)
My, what a charmer; what a sweet young thing!
Why are you muttering so? Fairest of creatures,
Let me remove your mask and see your features!

TRUFALDIN

Be off, you vicious knaves! Get out of my sight,
You wretches! And you, sir, thank you and good night.

(Exit Trufaldin.)

LÉLIE

(Having unmasked Mascarille.)
Mascarille, is it you?

MASCARILLE

No, it's someone else entirely.

LÉLIE

What a shock! Alas, fate's treated me most direly.
Since you'd told me nothing, how could I surmise
That you were hidden under that disguise?
Poor botcher that I am, it makes me sick
Unwittingly to have played you such a trick.
So angry am I that I'd like to whack
Myself a thousand times across my back.

MASCARILLE

Farewell, fine schemer, cleverest of men.

LÉLIE

If you're too enraged to help me ever again,
Then who will guide me?

MASCARILLE

Satan will do that for you.

LÉLIE

Oh, if you don't yet hate me, I implore you
Once more to pardon my stupidities!
If I must kiss your feet, or clasp your knees,
I'll gladly . . .

MASCARILLE

Nonsense. Come, my lads, I hear
Another band of revelers drawing near.

Scene 9

Léandre and his company (masked), Trufaldin (at his window).

LÉANDRE

No noise, now; let's be proper and polite.

TRUFALDIN

What! Throngs of masquers at my door all night?
Don't catch a cold for nothing, sirs; take care;
You're going to have a good long wait out there.
It's a little late for carrying off Célie,
Who offers her regrets, by way of me.
She's gone to bed, and cannot see you now,
But, wishing to express her thanks somehow
For all your kind solicitude and pains,
She sends you what this fragrant pot contains.

LÉANDRE

Oh no, I'm soaked! And what an awful stink!
Let's go, my friends; they're on to us, I think.

Act Four

Scene 1

Lélie (disguised as an Armenian), Mascarille.

MASCARILLE
In that weird garb, you're the prettiest thing alive.

LÉLIE
Your new scheme makes my fainting hopes revive.

MASCARILLE
I can't stay angry; my wrath is quickly spent.
I rage, and then, as always, I relent.

LÉLIE
My friend, if ever I come into my own,
My gratitude will lavishly be shown.
And while I have one crust of bread to share—

MASCARILLE

Enough. You have a part, now, to prepare.
This time, you have a role to memorize,
And can't claim to be taken by surprise
If you should blunder, and spoil another plan.

LÉLIE

You're living now, you say, with Trufaldin?

MASCARILLE

Yes. I feigned a deep concern for the old duffer,
And warned him to be careful lest he suffer
From plots and strategies his foes were hatching.
Two parties, so I said, were bent on snatching
The slave regarding whom he'd just received
A letter too absurd to be believed.
They had, I said, attempted to enlist
My aid, but it was easy to resist,
Because I loved him so, and would not hurt him,
And felt it was my duty to alert him.
I then held forth on how deceit and fraud,
In these dark days, walk brazenly abroad;
How I'd grown weary of the worldly life
And, wishing to withdraw from sin and strife
So as to mend my soul, had formed a plan
To dwell beneath the roof of some good man.
I added that, if he were willing, I'd
Rejoice to live with him until I died;
That my devotion to him was so fervent
That I'd expect no wages as his servant;
That I'd entrust to his wise custody
My savings and my father's legacy;
And that, if Heaven called me to my rest,
He would inherit all that I possessed.

That last thought won his heart, needless to say.
My aim in all this was to find a way
For you and your beloved to rendezvous
In secret, and determine what to do;
But I was led to think how you might be
Admitted to her house quite openly,
When, speaking of a long-lost son, he said
That he'd seen him, in a dream, rise from the dead.
Now, here's the history which he then related,
And on which our new hoax is predicated.

LÉLIE

I know all that; you've told me twice before.

MASCARILLE

Yes, yes; and though I tell it all once more,
It may be that your great mind still will fail
To recollect some critical detail.

LÉLIE

I cannot bear to stand around and stall.

MASCARILLE

Let's not be hasty, or we may trip and fall.
Your brain, sir, is a little thick and slow;
Learn your part cold, and then we'll have our show.
'Twas from Naples, you'll recall, that Trufaldin came.
Zanobio Ruberti was then his name.
It was suspected (though he's not the sort
To topple governments) that he'd lent support
To some insurgents of the left or right,
And so he had to flee the town by night.
His wife and infant daughter were left behind,
And he soon heard, with great distress of mind,
That they were dead. Alone and much cast down,

He wished to take his wealth to some new town
And buy a house, and live there with his one
Remaining child—Horace, a dear young son.
He wrote a letter to Bologna, where
The boy was being schooled by one Albert,
And sadly waited while, for two years' space,
None came to the appointed meeting place.
At last he judged that they were dead, and so
Moved to this city, and took the name we know,
And has in twelve years had no word, alas,
Of this Albert or of the son, Horace.
There's the tale, retold in a manner brief and broad,
To help you grasp the groundwork of our fraud.
Now, you're an Armenian merchant, and you're to tell
Of seeing those two in Turkey—alive and well,
As Trufaldin predicted in his dream.
I chose that fiction for our little scheme,
Since folk are often, in romantic works,
Kidnapped at sea by buccaneering Turks,
Are thought to be dead for fifteen years or more,
Then turn up smiling at their kinfolks' door.
I've read a hundred stories in that vein.
Let's steal the plot; 'twill save us mental strain.
So—you're to tell how the two men had been sold
As slaves; and how you ransomed them with gold;
And how, when you left because of urgent news,
Horace asked you to see his father, whose
Address he'd lately learned, and linger here
For a few days until they should appear.
Have you followed that long-winded exposition?

LÉLIE

It's pointless, all this boring repetition.
I understood it all the first time through.

MASCARILLE

Then I'll go in, and prepare the way for you.

LÉLIE

Wait, Mascarille. There's one small thing, just one:
What if he asks me to describe his son?

MASCARILLE

Why should that be a problem? After all,
His son, when last he saw him, was very small.
And can we not assume, in any case,
That time and slavery have transformed his face?

LÉLIE

That's true. But . . . if he remembers seeing me,
What shall I do?

MASCARILLE

Have you no memory?
I've said already that your features can
Have made no real impression on Trufaldin,
Since you so briefly passed before his eyes.
What's more, your beard and clothes are a fine disguise.

LÉLIE

All right . . . But where, in Turkey, shall I claim . . . ?

MASCARILLE

Turkey or Barbary, it's all the same.

LÉLIE

But where did I see them? What's the name of the town?

MASCARILLE

Tunis! He'll keep me here till the sun goes down.
He says my repetitions are a bore,
But he's made me name that town ten times or more.

LÉLIE

Go in, then, and prepare the way; I'm ready.

MASCARILLE

Now, do act prudently; be staid and steady.
None of your Spanish inspirations, please.

LÉLIE

Don't worry. You have such strange anxieties!

MASCARILLE

Horace—schooled in Bologna. Trufaldin—
Zanobio Ruberti in Naples, where he began—
Albert the tutor . . .

LÉLIE

It sounds like grammar school
When you drill me so; do you take me for a fool?

MASCARILLE

No, just a little retarded, so to speak.

LÉLIE

(Alone:)
When I don't require his help, he's mild and meek,
But when he knows I need him, as at present,
His tongue grows disrespectful and unpleasant.
Ah, soon she'll turn those radiant eyes on me
Which hold me in such sweet captivity;
Soon I'll be free to let that fair one know,

In burning words, what pains I undergo,
And learn from her my fate . . . But here they are.

Scene 2

Trufaldin, Lélie, Mascarille.

TRUFALDIN

Praise be to Heaven, and to my lucky star!

MASCARILLE

You're good at "seeing visions and dreaming dreams,"
Since what you dream about comes true, it seems.

TRUFALDIN

(To Lélie:)
For these good tidings, how can I thank you, sir?
You seem to me a heavenly messenger.

LÉLIE

Spare me such compliments, I beg of you.

TRUFALDIN

(To Mascarille:)
I don't know where, but I've seen someone who
Resembles this Armenian.

MASCARILLE

It's the same with me:
It's eerie how alike some men can be.

TRUFALDIN

So you've seen the son on whom my fond hopes rest?

LÉLIE

Oh, yes, signor, he's hale and full of zest.

TRUFALDIN

Did he speak of me, when he told you of his fate?

LÉLIE

Oh, a thousand times!

MASCARILLE

(Aside to Lélie:)
                    Let's not exaggerate.

LÉLIE

He described you to me, just as I see you now:
Your face, your bearing . . .

TRUFALDIN

He did? I don't see how.
He was but seven when he saw me last.
Even his tutor, since so much time has passed,
Would find it hard to recognize my face.

MASCARILLE

From a son's deep memory, nothing can erase
His father's image, and in that sense bereave him;
My own dear father . . .

TRUFALDIN

                    Enough.
(To Lélie:)
Where did you leave him?

LÉLIE

At Turin, in Turkey.

TRUFALDIN

Turin? But that town
Is in Piedmont, surely?

MASCARILLE

(Aside:)

Oh, that brainless clown!
(To Trufaldin:)
You misunderstand, sir; *Tunis,* he means to say.
That's where he left your son the other day.
Armenians have some odd pronunciations
Which jar upon the ears of other nations:
They voice the syllable *nis* as *rin*, and thus
When they say "Tunis," it sounds like "Turin" to us.

TRUFALDIN

Such a curious fact was more than I could guess.
(To Lélie:)
How did you find me? Did he give you my address?

MASCARILLE

(Aside:)
Will the idiot never answer?
*(Mascarille makes urgent signals to Lélie, and when this is noticed by
Trufaldin, pretends to be fencing.)*
I was just
Rehearsing a little bit of cut and thrust.
I used to be a champion at that sport,
And shone in fencing bouts of every sort.

TRUFALDIN

(To Mascarille:)
Fencing is not my present interest.
(To Lélie:)
What other name did he say I had possessed?

89

MASCARILLE

Ah, Signor Zanobio Ruberti, what a joy
That Heaven's restored to you your cherished boy!

LÉLIE

That's your real name; the other's a pseudonym.

TRUFALDIN

And where was he born? Did you learn that, too, from him?

MASCARILLE

Naples would seem a charming place to live,
Though your memories must be dark and negative.

TRUFALDIN

Can't you be still and let us talk, my man?

LÉLIE

It was in Naples that his life began.

TRUFALDIN

Where was he sent as a child, and in whose care?

MASCARILLE

You should think highly of the good Albert;
After Bologna, he stayed at your son's side,
Still serving as his guardian and his guide.

TRUFALDIN

Humph!

MASCARILLE

(*Aside:*)
  If this goes on much longer, we're undone.

TRUFALDIN

Tell me what happened to him and to my son;
When Fate surprised them, what vessel were they on?

MASCARILLE

It's strange, I can't do anything but yawn.
Come, Signor Trufaldin, don't you think it meet
That your foreign guest be given a bite to eat?
It's growing late.

LÉLIF

No thank you; nothing for me.

MASCARILLE

You're hungrier than you think, sir. Wait and see.

TRUFALDIN

Come in, then.

LÉLIE

After you.

MASCARILLE

In Armenia, sir,
The host goes in before the visitor.
(To Lélie, after Trufaldin has gone into the house:)
You poor thing! Can't you speak?

LÉLIE

I was at first
Flustered, and so forgot what we'd rehearsed.
But now, don't worry, I shall talk a lot . . .

MASCARILLE

Here comes your rival, who doesn't suspect our plot.

Scene 3

Anselme, Léandre.

ANSELME

Wait, Léandre. I've some counsels to impart
That have your honor and peace of mind at heart.
I don't come as the father of Hippolyte,
To urge you for our sake to be discreet;
Rather I speak as your dear father would,
If he gave you frank advice for your own good,
Or as I'd wish some man, with kindly suasion,
To advise my own son, were there a like occasion.
D'you know what the town's been saying since last night,
When this amour of yours first came to light?—
To what coarse gossip, sneers and winking eyes
Your last night's escapade has given rise?—
What people think of your capricious taste
In choosing for your lady an unchaste
Gypsy, a woman of the streets, a jade
Whose noblest calling is the beggar's trade?
I blush for you; and for myself no less,
Who am involved in this opprobrious mess:
For if my daughter, whom you courted, were
Forsaken, 'twould insult both me and her.
Léandre, my boy, put all of this behind you!
Don't let infatuation further blind you.
No man is always wise; we've all transgressed;
But the shortest errors always are the best.
When a wife brings only beauty as her dower,
One's marriage soon grows needy, cold and sour,
And the wife's pretty face cannot contend
With the gloom in which such hasty matches end.
No, I repeat, these rash and starry-eyed

Weddings, these ardent unions, can provide
A few sweet nights of passion, to be sure;
But such felicities do not endure.
Once it is gratified, desire decays,
And those sweet nights give way to bitter days—
To cares and miseries, to frets and bothers,
And sons cut off by their indignant fathers.

LÉANDRE
In what you've said, there's nothing I've not heard
From my own conscience, almost word for word.
For the honor you would do me, I'm your debtor,
And I shall strive, sir, to deserve it better.
Though passion still would blind me, I now see
Your daughter's worth and virtue beckoning me,
And I'm determined—

ANSELME
That door is opening! Come,
Let's get away from here, for fear that some
Black magic from that house will seize your soul.

Scene 4

Lélie, Mascarille.

MASCARILLE
If you keep on making dumb mistakes, our whole
Conspiracy will crumble in our hands.

LÉLIE
Why must I hear these endless reprimands?
What have I done? Didn't I get things right
Once we had gone inside the house?

MASCARILLE

Not quite.
You said that the Turks are heretics, and swore
With utter certainty that they adore
The sun and moon as their ancestral gods.
Well, let that pass. What's crazier, by all odds,
Is the moonstruck way you act around Célie.
Your love is like a simmering fricassee,
Which, when the fire beneath it gets too hot,
Comes bubbling up and overflows the pot.

LÉLIE

My coolness and restraint were infinite!
I hardly spoke to her, you must admit.

MASCARILLE

You hardly spoke, but how you did behave!
During our brief repast, your actions gave
More reason for suspicion than, I fear,
Another man could give in half a year.

LÉLIE

How so?

MASCARILLE

How so? When Trufaldin asked Célie
To join us at the table, all could see
How your enchanted gaze was fixed on her.
Blushing and mute and lovesick as you were,
You left your food untouched, and had no thirst,
Unless she took a sip of claret first;
Then you would seize her glass with eager will,
Not letting any drop of liquid spill,
And drink whatever wine remained within,

Placing your lips where her two lips had been.
Each scrap of bread that she had touched or bitten
You pounced upon as quickly as a kitten
That seeks to pin a mouse beneath its paw,
And popped them all into your greedy maw.
Under the table, furthermore, your feet
Kept up a jittery annoying beat
And Trufaldin, whom you twice kicked in the shins,
Punished two blameless puppies for your sins,
Because they couldn't speak and clear their name.
Was all this wise behavior, as you claim?
Watching you made me twist and squirm and get,
Despite the season, into a burning sweat.
I watched you as a man who plays at bowls
Studies his ball's trajectory as it rolls,
And, like that man, I writhed and twitched, as though
I could control your folly by doing so.

LÉLIE

My passionate acts are easy to condemn,
Since you're not in love with what occasions them!
Still, for your sake, I'll try now to subdue
The amorous seizures that I'm subject to.
I'll . . .

Scene 5

Trufaldin, Lélie, Mascarille.

MASCARILLE

We were speaking of your son's adversities.

TRUFALDIN

That's kind of you.
(*To Lélie:*)
Will you permit me, please,
To have a private word with Mascarille?

LÉLIE

I'll gladly do you, sir, that courtesy.

(*Lélie goes into Trufaldin's house.*)

TRUFALDIN

Now, listen: Do you know what I've just done?

MASCARILLE

I don't, sir; but the odds are ten to one
That you'll soon tell me.

TRUFALDIN

From a great oak, tall and strong,
Whose mighty life is now two centuries long,
I cut a handsome branch, selecting it
Because it had the largeness requisite.
Of it I fashioned, with much skill and quickness,
(*Holding out his arm.*)
A cudgel of . . . let's see . . . about this thickness,
Though tapered at one end. A single whack
From it's worth fifty lashes on the back,
Because it's heavy, and full of knots as well.

MASCARILLE

For whose sake have you done all this, pray tell?

TRUFALDIN

For you, first; then for that most pious brother
Who'd foist one person on me, and filch another—
That rascal in Armenian disguise
Who took me in with a damned pack of lies.

MASCARILLE

What! You don't think . . .

TRUFALDIN

There's nothing you can say,
For he himself has given the game away:
He whispered to Célie, squeezing her hand,
That for her sake his wicked hoax was planned—
Not knowing that Jeannette, my godchild, heard
The whole confession, missing not a word.
He didn't mention you, but I've no doubt
That you were in cahoots with him throughout.

MASCARILLE

Oh, sir, you wrong me. If he imposed on you,
He fooled me first. I thought his tale was true.

TRUFALDIN

If you want to prove to me that you're sincere,
Then help me throw that scoundrel out of here.
Once we have banged and battered him a little,
I shall bestow on you a full acquittal.

MASCARILLE

I'll gladly thrash him, and prove that I did not
Have any part in this distasteful plot.
(Aside:)
Yes, you Armenian ass, you're going to pay
For this last bungle!

Scene 6

Lélie, Trufaldin, Mascarille.

TRUFALDIN

(To Lélie, having knocked at his door:)
        Come out and join us, pray.
So, you impostor! Do you dare deceive
An honest man with cruel make-believe . . .

MASCARILLE

Pretending to have seen his son abroad,
So as to get into his house by fraud?

TRUFALDIN

(Beating Lélie.)
Be off, this minute!

LÉLIE

(To Mascarille, who is also beating him:)
        Ah, you knave!

MASCARILLE

      It's thus
That tricksters . . .

LÉLIE

Villain!

MASCARILLE

     Are chastised by us.
Take that!

LÉLIE

Shall a gentleman be knocked about . . . ?

MASCARILLE

I'll knock your head off, if you don't clear out.

TRUFALDIN

Well done. Come, let's go in. I'm satisfied.

LÉLIE

(*Returning.*)
Thrashed by my own valet! I'm mortified.
Who would have thought the flunky could betray
His master in so insolent a way?

MASCARILLE

(*From Trufaldin's window.*)
If you don't mind my asking, how's your back?

LÉLIE

You dare address me, after that base attack?

MASCARILLE

I've no apologies. It's what you get
For babbling, and not noticing Jeannette.
But I won't rage against you now. For once
I shan't blow up and curse you for a dunce;
Though what you did was rash and asinine,
I've taken out my anger on your spine.

LÉLIE

I'll have revenge for that disloyal act!

MASCARILLE

You brought that beating on yourself, in fact.

LÉLIE

I? How?

MASCARILLE

If you had used your wits in there,
When you were talking with your lady fair,
You would have seen the young Jeannette draw near
And drink in all you said with eager ear.

LÉLIE

That I was overheard, I can't conceive.

MASCARILLE

Why, then, were you so brusquely asked to leave?
No, no, your loose tongue gave our game away.
I'd hate to see you try to play piquet:
You'd show your hand and lose, again and again.

LÉLIE

Oh, I'm the most unfortunate of men!
But why did you join our host in beating me?

MASCARILLE

It was the brainy thing to do, lest he
Suspect that I had framed our plot, or deem
That I'd been your accomplice in the scheme.

LÉLIE

You could at least have beaten me more gently.

MASCARILLE

No. Trufaldin was watching me intently:
Besides, I rather relished an excuse
To turn my anger and frustration loose.
But now, what's done is done. If you will state
Your solemn promise not to retaliate—
Either directly or more roundaboutly—
For the blows I rained upon your back so stoutly,
I shall exploit my situation here,
And in two days gain for you your captive dear.

LÉLIE

My back still feels resentful, but you've made me
An offer which is certain to persuade me!

MASCARILLE

You give your word, then?

LÉLIE

Yes, I promise you.

MASCARILLE

Promise me, too, that in whatever I do
You will no longer interfere and blunder.

LÉLIE

Agreed.

MASCARILLE

You'd better keep your word, by thunder!

LÉLIE

Keep yours and help me win the best of maids.

MASCARILLE

Go rub some ointment on your shoulder blades.

LÉLIE

(Alone:)

Why is it that misfortune dogs me so?

Why am I visited by woe on woe?

MASCARILLE

(Emerging from Trufaldin's house.)

What! Haven't you gone? Be off now, in a hurry.

Leave everything to me; it's not your worry.

I shall be working for you, and you must never

Attempt to help in any way whatever.

Go home; do nothing.

LÉLIE

(Leaving.)

All right, then. Count on me.

MASCARILLE

Now to conceive a brand-new strategy.

Scene 7

Ergaste, Mascarille.

ERGASTE

Wait, Mascarille. I have some news that seems

A bitter setback for your hopes and schemes.

Even as I speak, a fine young gypsy man,

Well bred and fair, is seeking Trufaldin,

Accompanied by a crone with trembling chin.

He's come to buy that slave you'd hoped to win,
And speaks of her in tones of anxious love.

MASCARILLE

No doubt, he's the swain Célie has told me of.
In this affair, what endless trials we face!
When one threat fades, another takes its place.
What matter that Léandre, so they claim,
Will now give up Célie and quit the game;
That his father's come to town, has judged it meet
And proper that his son wed Hippolyte,
And has so moved Léandre to obey
That the marriage contract's to be signed today?
One rival's gone; but another far more dire
Has come to rob us of our heart's desire.
However, by a bit of brilliant guile
I shall prevent their leaving for a while,
And thus allow myself some time to spend
On bringing things to a triumphant end.
There've been some unsolved robberies of late;
Theft is a crime that gypsies perpetrate;
I'll cleverly arrange that on a frail
Suspicion, this fellow shall be thrown in jail.
I know some officers, full of zeal and zest,
Who're always glad to make a false arrest;
They find it a most profitable sport,
Because of the little bribes they can extort;
The suspect may be innocent, but they
Regard his purse as guilty, and make it pay.

Act Five

Scene 1

Mascarille, Ergaste.

MASCARILLE

You ape! You ox! You blockhead! Must you forever
Subvert my every project and endeavor?

ERGASTE

Your friends the officers did their duty well,
And nabbed the gypsy. He'd now be in a cell,
Had not your master, happening on the scene,
Been furiously moved to intervene.
"To see a gentleman so abused," he cried,
"Is a shameful thing which I shall not abide.
Release him! I'm prepared to stand his bail."
When still they sought to drag their prey to jail,
Your master fell upon those paladins

So fiercely that they ran to save their skins.
No doubt they're running yet, and each one feels
That a wild Lélie is close upon his heels.

MASCARILLE

He doesn't know, poor fool, that the gypsy's there
Inside, about to steal his lady fair.

ERGASTE

I'm off. A bit of pressing business calls me.

MASCARILLE

(Alone:)
Alas, this latest feat of his appalls me.
It might be said (and I might well attest)
That the meddling imp by which he is possessed
Delights in balking me, and prompting him
To do whatever makes our chances dim.
Still, I shall not abandon our campaign.
We'll see who wins—his devil, or my brain.
Célie is rather fond of him, and so
Is far from feeling a desire to go.
I'll seek to take advantage of that fact.
But now they're coming, and it's time to act.
That house across the way is mine to use,
For our good cause, in any way I choose.
I'm the custodian, and I keep the key.
All will be well, if fortune favors me.
Oh, my! What a busy day or two I've spent!
How many tricks a scoundrel must invent!

Scene 2

Célie, Andrès.

ANDRÈS

I have done everything a man could do,
Célie, to prove my ardent love to you.
When I dwelt in Venice, in my younger days,
My courage as a soldier won me praise,
And, not to boast, I might have had a very
Distinguished future in the military.
But that, and everything, I could dismiss
When, in a sudden metamorphosis,
I came to be your rapt adorer, and
A fellow wanderer in your gypsy band,
Who followed you in spite of strange events
And adverse fates, and your indifference.
Of late, when we by chance were separated
For a longer time than I'd anticipated,
I spared no pains to learn where you had flown;
At last a gypsy woman, an ancient crone,
Relieved my anxious heart by telling me
That you'd been left here as security
For monies that your band had had to borrow
To save themselves from penury and sorrow.
I've hastened here to free you, and I stand
In readiness to obey your least command,
Though disappointed that your eyes express
A pensive gloom instead of happiness.
If you would like a settled life, then come—
I can support us both in Venice, from
My portion of the spoils we took in war;
Or if you wish to wander, as before,

I'll gladly follow; my heart's one craving, now,
Is to be near to you, no matter how.

CÉLIE

Your kindly zeal is most apparent to me;
I'd be ungrateful if it made me gloomy.
The fact is that my face does not reveal,
At the present moment, what I truly feel.
It's a fierce headache that makes me frown this way;
And if I can command you, as you say,
I'd like our voyage hence to be suspended,
For a few days, until this pain is ended.

ANDRÈS

We'll put it off as long as you require.
To please you is the one thing I desire.
Let's find a place where you can stay and rest.
That house, it seems, will take a paying guest.

(He points to a ROOMS TO LET sign which Mascarille has just put in the window.)

Scene 3

Célie, Andrès, Mascarille (disguised as a Swiss).

ANDRÈS

Ah, the landlord. You are Swiss, sir, one presumes.

MASCARILLE

Ja, at your serfice.

ANDRÈS

May we engage some rooms?

MASCARILLE

For strainchers, I haf goot accomodations,
But not for doze mit vicked reputations.

ANDRÈS

Your house is free, I'm sure, of wickedness.

MASCARILLE

You vas a straincher in diss city, yes?

ANDRÈS

Yes.

MASCARILLE

De mattam, she iss married to de mister?

ANDRÈS

What?

MASCARILLE

She iss your vife, or maype iss your schvister?

ANDRÈS

No.

MASCARILLE

Ach, she iss pooty. You come on piziness, eh?
Maype you bring a zoot in court today?
Lawzoot is one bad sing, it cost zo much.
De lawyer iss a tief, zo iss de jutch.

ANDRÈS

We have no lawsuit.

MASCARILLE

Den you bring her here mit you
To valk aroundt de city, und zee de fiew?

ANDRÈS

Yes, yes.
(To Célie:)
I'll let you rest a bit, my dear,
While I bring the ancient gypsy woman here,
And countermand the carriage that I hired.

MASCARILLE

She's not vell?

ANDRÈS

She has a headache, and is tired.

MASCARILLE

I haf goot vine, also I haf goot cheece.
Enter my little dvellink, if you pleece.

(Célie, Andrès and Mascarille go into the house.)

Scene 4

Lélie, Andrès.

LÉLIE

(Alone:)
Impatient as my heart may be, I swore
That I would take no action anymore.
My man shall act alone, and I must wait
To see how Heaven will decide my fate.

(To Andrès, who is coming out of the house:)
Were you seeking someone in that building, pray?

ANDRÈS

No, it's an inn, where I've arranged to stay.

LÉLIE

What! My father owns that house, and the fact is
That my man sleeps there, and guards the premises.

ANDRÈS

Well, that placard plainly offers rooms for rent.
Read it.

LÉLIE

It does! I'm filled with wonderment.
Who in the deuce would put it there, and why?
Ah! I've a notion where the truth may lie!
There's just one answer to this mystery.

ANDRÈS

May I presume to ask what that may be?

LÉLIE

From all but you, I'd guard this secret well.
But you're not involved, and I know you wouldn't tell.
I have no doubt that the placard you behold—
At least, I think so—is another bold
Prank by the man of whom I just made mention,
Part of some deft intrigue of his invention,
Designed to put me in possession of
A gypsy girl whom I intensely love.
We've not yet gained her, though we've tried no end.

ANDRÈS

What's her name?

LÉLIE

Célie.

ANDRÈS

If you'd told me earlier, friend,
I could have spared you all the pains it took
To think up this deceit, and bait the hook.

LÉLIE

How so? Do you know her?

ANDRÈS

'Twas I who just now bought
Her freedom.

LÉLIE

You did? I'm staggered by the thought.

ANDRÈS

She wasn't well enough to travel, and thus
I'd just engaged—in there—some rooms for us.
Well, I'm delighted that you've told me, sir,
Of your intentions with regard to her.

LÉLIE

What! Will you cause my cup to overflow
By helping me to gain her?

ANDRÈS

(Knocking on the door.)
　　　　You soon shall know.

LÉLIE

How can I ever thank you for this kind . . .

ANDRÈS

No, no, let's have no thanks, if you don't mind.

Scene 5

Lélie, Andrès, Mascarille.

MASCARILLE

(*Aside:*)
Ohh! What do I see but my demented master?
Now, I am sure, we'll have some new disaster.

LÉLIE

Well, Mascarille! No one would ever guess
That it was you in that outlandish dress.

MASCARILLE

Vy do you call me Mackerel? I don't vish
Zat you make fun of me und call me fish.

LÉLIE

Ha! What delightful gibberish you talk!

MASCARILLE

Schtop laughing at me; go take yourself a valk.

LÉLIE

Come, I'm your master; let's play this game no more.

MASCARILLE

By Himmel, I neffer zee your face before.

LÉLIE

It's all been settled; drop all these droll pretenses.

MASCARILLE

If you von't go, I knock you from your senses.

LÉLIE

Stop talking German, I tell you; there's no need.
This generous man and I are fully agreed.
I am to have the thing I hold most dear,
And you've no grounds for diffidence or fear.

MASCARILLE

If you're so happily agreed, I'll then
De-Swiss myself, and be myself again.

ANDRÈS

Your man has served you with great zeal and wit.
I'll soon rejoin you; kindly wait a bit.

(Andrès goes into the house.)

LÉLIE

Well! What do you say?

MASCARILLE

I say that I'm completely
Happy to see our labors end so sweetly.

LÉLIE

You were rather slow to shed your Swiss disguise,
And you heard my glorious news with doubtful eyes.

MASCARILLE

Knowing you as I do, I felt uneasy,
And your blithe report still leaves me feeling queasy.

LÉLIE

Oh, come! Confess that I have done great things:
This makes up for my former blunderings,
And crowns with victory our joint campaign.

MASCARILLE

You may be right: With luck, who needs a brain?

Scene 6

Célie, Andrès, Lélie, Mascarille.

ANDRÈS

Is this the lady of whom you spoke, of late?

LÉLIE

What bliss so sweet as mine, what joy so great!

ANDRÈS

I owe you thanks for a gallant deed, I know;
Not to acknowledge it would be base and low:
Yet it would be too harsh a recompense
If I repaid you at my heart's expense.
Without this beautiful lady, I'd be lost.
Would you have me pay my debt at such a cost?
No, you're too generous. Farewell. Our plans
Are to spend a day or two at Trufaldin's.

(He exits with Célie.)

MASCARILLE

(After singing for some time.)
I laugh and sing, but in truth I feel no glee.
You're "fully agreed"! He's giving you Célie!
Well, I needn't say it.

LÉLIE

This is too much! I'm through
Begging your aid, and botching all you do.
I'm an oaf, a ninny, a bumbling blatherskite,
Unworthy of help, unable to do things right.
Go; cease to serve a fool who hates success,
And fends off every chance of happiness.
After my mad mistakes in word and deed,
Death is the only helper that I need.

(Exit.)

MASCARILLE

(Alone:)
Yes, that would be a perfect finishing touch;
Nothing adorns a foolish life so much
As a good suicide in the finale.
But I won't let his rage at his own folly
Lead him to throw my services away.
In spite of him, I'll serve him. Come what may,
I'll best the devil that makes him blunder so.
It's noble to confront so stubborn a foe,
And all one's trials are but handmaids who
Adorn one's virtue in high Heaven's view.

Scene 7

Célie, Mascarílle.

CÉLIE
(To Mascarílle, who has been whispering to her:)
Whatever anyone may do or say,
Little, I think, will come of this delay.
By what just happened, we can see how far
From any compromise the two men are,
And, as I've told you, I couldn't bear to make
One man unhappy for the other's sake.
To each of them, for different reasons, I
Feel bound by a profound and potent tie.
Lélie has by the power of love subdued
My heart, but Andrès has my gratitude,
Which bars me, even in my secret mind,
From any course which he would think unkind.
Yes, if I cannot grant his heart's desire,
And meet his ardor with an answering fire,
I can at least, in view of all he's done,
Refuse to give my hand to anyone,
And let my amorous wishes be suppressed
As painfully as those that he's professed.
You see what honor forces me to do,
And what faint hopes I can hold out to you.

MASCARILLE
The hopes you give are faint indeed, that's clear,
And I don't deal in miracles, I fear.
But I'll make use of every skill I've learned—
Move earth and Heaven, leave no stone unturned—
To find some exit from this cul-de-sac.
As soon as I've news to bring you, I'll be back.

Scene 8

Hippolyte, Célie.

HIPPOLYTE
Since you came here, madam, the ladies of these parts
Have learned to fear your eyes, which steal men's hearts;
Their cherished conquests have been lost to you;
Their lovers, one and all, are now untrue.
There is no man, it seems, who stands a chance
Before the lovely arrows of your glance,
And, every day, our losses are your gains,
As free men, by the score, put on your chains.
As for myself, I would have seen no harm
In the sovereign power of your wondrous charm
If, when you took my lovers from me, you'd
Spared me just one to warm my solitude;
But since you inhumanely left me none,
I feel I must complain of what you've done.

CÉLIE
Madam, how charmingly you chaff and tease;
But do have pity on me, if you please.
Your own eyes know their power far too well
To fear that such as I could break their spell;
They are too conscious of their loveliness
To harbor such alarms as you express.

HIPPOLYTE
Yet when I said that you purloin our beaus,
I only said what everybody knows;
Léandre and Lélie, to name but two,
Are well known to have lost their hearts to you.

CÉLIE

If there is truth in that report about them,
I'm sure that you will gladly do without them,
For any errant lover who has shown
Such wretched taste can hardly please your own.

HIPPOLYTE

Ah, no. Indeed, I feel quite otherwise.
Your beauty is so stunning in my eyes
That I can see good reason to acquit
A straying lover who's been stunned by it.
I cannot blame Léandre who, when he
Beheld your face, forgot his vows to me,
And I'll receive him without rancor when,
At his sire's insistence, he is mine again.

Scene 9

Célie, Hippolyte, Mascarille.

MASCARILLE

Great news! Good tidings! Harken to my voice,
And I shall give you reason to rejoice!

CÉLIE

Quick! Tell us!

MASCARILLE

Hear me; this is going to be . . .

CÉLIE

What?

MASCARILLE

Like the ending of a comedy.
Just now, that ancient gypsy woman . . .

CÉLIE

Yes! Hurry!

MASCARILLE

Was strolling through the square, without a worry,
When another hag, who had been keeping pace
With her, and closely studying her face,
Burst into loud reproaches, screamed and swore,
And gave the signal for a bloody war.
'Twas not with sword or musket that they fought,
But with four withered claws, whereby they sought
To pick each other clean, those scrawny crones,
Of the little flesh still clinging to their bones.
Such words as "slut" and "vixen" filled the air.
Their bonnets soon flew off, and thus laid bare
A couple of bald heads, so that the twosome
Composed a battle scene both droll and gruesome.
Andrès and Trufaldin, who were in the van
Of a crowd that gathered when the fray began,
Found it no easy task to separate
Two combatants whose anger was so great.
When the storm abated, and each of them had sped
To cover up the bareness of her head,
And the crowd was asking what had caused the brawl,
The strange old woman who'd begun it all,
Though still much agitated and inflamed,
Looked fixedly at Trufaldin, and exclaimed:
"It's you, sir, of whom I heard not long ago
That you were living here *incognito*!
Yes, yes, it's you! O wondrous circumstance!

Signor Zanobio Ruberti, by happy chance
I've found you just when I'd begun to take
A vigorous course of action for your sake.
When you left Naples and your family,
I was your little daughter's nurse, and she
At four possessed a charm and grace which were
Remarkable, as you'll remember, sir.
The vile hag whom you see there wormed her way
Into our household till, one bitter day,
She stole my precious charge. Alas, your wife
Was seized by deepest sorrow, and her life
Was shortened by a loss she could not bear.
Since the child had been abducted from my care,
I feared your wrath, and had you notified
That both the mother and the child had died.
But let's compel this woman, now that I've caught her,
To tell us what has happened to your daughter."
At the name "Zanobio Ruberti," which occurred
A number of times in the long speech we heard,
Andrès turned pale, and then at last began
This speech to the astonished Trufaldin:
"Thank Heaven, which has helped me to regain
The sire whom, until now, I sought in vain!
How strange that, seeing you, I was unseeing,
And did not know the author of my being!
Yes, Father, I am Horace, your long-lost son.
When Albert died, who'd been my guardian,
A restless mood came over me, and I
Forsook Bologna, put my studies by,
And, driven by my curiosity,
Wandered for six years over land and sea,
Until, in time, I felt a secret yen
To see my kindred and my home again.
Alas, in Naples, Father, I could not find you,

And since you'd gone, and left no trail behind you,
I ceased my wanderings and my fruitless quest,
Settled in Venice, and was a while at rest.
From that time to the present, I have known
Nought of our family but the name alone."
I leave you to imagine with what bliss
Trufaldin lent an ear to all of this.
But to be brief—since you can learn with ease
Whatever further history you may please—
Trufaldin, having heard the gypsy crone
Confess, has recognized you as his own;
Andrès, then, is your brother; and since a brother
And sister cannot marry one another,
He would repay an act of chivalry
By yielding you in marriage to Lélie.
My master's father, who was there, concurred,
And gave his warm consent—then, feeling stirred
To make a grand occasion still more grand,
Gave the new-found Horace his daughter's hand.
Was there ever such a blizzard of events?

CÉLIE

I'm overwhelmed by these developments.

MASCARILLE

Everyone's bound this way, save those two hags,
Who need to rest from battle, and mend their rags.
(To Hippolyte:)
Léandre's coming, and your father as well.
As for myself, I'll go in haste and tell
My downcast master that his luck in love
Has been restored, as if by Heaven above.

(Exit.)

HIPPOLYTE

I'm overcome with joy, and couldn't be
More joyous if these things had happened to me.
But here they come.

Scene 10

Trufaldin, Anselme, Pandolfe, Célie, Hippolyte, Léandre, Andrès.

TRUFALDIN

My daughter!

CÉLIE

Father dear!

TRUFALDIN

Has the news of all our blessings reached you here?

CÉLIE

Yes, the whole astounding story has been told.

HIPPOLYTE

(To Léandre, gesturing toward Célie:)
No need to excuse yourself; my eyes behold
What might make any heart a renegade.

LÉANDRE

I beg your kind forgiveness for having strayed.
Believe me, it's not the urging of my sire
That brings me back to you, but my own desire.

ANDRÈS

(To Célie:)

Who would have thought that Nature could condemn
My fervor and my love, and banish them?
Yet since in them the purest honor reigned,
They shall, with slight adjustments, be retained.

CÉLIE

I long felt guilty, because I couldn't seem
To look on you with more than deep esteem.
I knew not what great obstacle kept my feet
From the path of love, so dangerous and sweet,
And warned me to deny the wild appeal
Of what my senses wished my heart to feel.

TRUFALDIN

(To Célie:)

Now that I've got you back, what would you say
If I thought at once of giving you away—
(Gesturing to Pandolfe.)
In marriage, to this gentleman's son? What say you?

CÉLIE

I'd say that I was bound, sir, to obey you.

Scene 11

Trufaldin, Anselme, Pandolfe, Célie, Hippolyte, Lélie, Léandre, Andrès, Mascarille.

MASCARILLE

(To Lélie:)

Let's see if your inner devil can destroy
A surefire prospect of delight and joy,

And if you will invent some more "fine schemes"
To block the realization of your dreams.
A wondrous turn of fortune now ensures
Your future happiness, and Célie is yours.

LÉLIE

Is it true? Has Heaven graciously decreed . . . ?

TRUFALDIN

It's true, my son-in-law.

PANDOLFE

We're all agreed.

ANDRÈS

In this, I gladly pay the debt I owe you.

LÉLIE

(To Mascarille:)
I'll give you a thousand hugs, dear man, to show you
My gratitude.

MASCARILLE

Oof! Please! Let go of me!
I'm suffocated. I fear for poor Célie
If, in your ardor, you embrace her so.
Such hugs as that I'm happy to forgo.

TRUFALDIN

(To Lélie:)
You know how Heaven has blessed me; but, my boy,
Since this one day has filled us all with joy,
Let's spend the rest together, and invite
Léandre's father to feast with us tonight.

MASCARILLE

So, you're all provided for. Is there no girl
Who'd like to give poor Mascarille a whirl?
Seeing these happy he's and she's converge
Has given me a sudden marrying urge.

ANSELME

I've a girl for you.

MASCARILLE

Then let's go—and through Heaven's graces
May all our children have their father's faces!

END OF PLAY

JEAN-BAPTISTE POQUELIN MOLIÈRE (1622–1673) was a French playwright and actor. Molière's plays include *The Misanthrope*, *Tartuffe*, *The School for Wives*, *The School for Husbands*, *The Miser*, *Lovers' Quarrels*, *The Imaginary Invalid* and *The Imaginary Cuckold, or Sganarelle*, among others.

RICHARD WILBUR is author of more than thirty-five books, including works of poetry, translation, prose, children's books and essays. Wilbur is the most prolific and gifted translator of Molière, and is credited with the explosive revival of Molière's plays in North America, beginning in 1955 with *The Misanthrope*. Wilbur's translations of Molière, Racine, Corneille and others are widely praised for incorporating the spirit of both language and author, while maintaining the original form and rhyme scheme. Wilbur is the only living American poet to have won the Pulitzer Prize twice. He has been awarded the National Book Award, the Bollingen Prize, two PEN translation awards and two Guggenheim fellowships. He served as U.S. Poet Laureate. Wilbur taught on the faculties of Harvard, Wellesley, Wesleyan and Smith (where he is poet emeritus). He lives in Cummington, Massachusetts, and is at present the Simpson Lecturer at Amherst College. His latest book of poetry *Anterooms: New Poems and Translations* (Houghton Mifflin Harcourt) will be published in November 2010.